# Guidance

# the Seeker of

# TRUTH

by Mark Zaretti

Second Edition

First Published © 2017

Second edition © 2019 The Way Back Group Ltd.
All Right Reserved

ISBN 978-1707871674

Books in The Way Back series
by Mark Zaretti:

Book 1.  Guidance for the Seeker of TRUTH
Second Edition

Book 2.  The Way Back, The Six Virtues

Coming soon:

Book 3.  The Way Back to TRUTH

Book 4.  The Way Back, Book of GRACE

There is nothingness, just completeness.

Because it is complete, everything is included
and nothing remains separate.

Having everything included it is all accepting
and so can be called "**Love**".

Because nothing is outside of it,
it has no edges and hence no limits.

Having no limits it can be called "**Limitless**".

Because it has no limit it has no size, it is simultaneously
infinitely small and infinitely large.

Because it is limitless, there is nowhere it is not
and so it has no location.

Because it is complete, it contains all locations
but is nowhere.

Because there is nowhere it is not already present,
it does not move.

Having no movement it can be called "**Stillness**"

Because there is no movement there is no time.

Because there is no time, there was never a time it was not
present, and so it is beyond time.

Having all times and being beyond time,
it can be called "**Eternal**".

Because it is eternal, there is nothing that came before it and so it
was not created.

Because it has no beginning, it has no end.

It does not know itself because there are no edges to perceive and no where from which to witness.

It is Love.  It is Stillness.  It is Eternal.

It simply IS.

From Love Grace creates a point.

Being something, this point has an edge.

Having an edge it is manifest.

Duality begins and there is an opposite point.

Each point is separate from the other.

There is now location and so the possibility of movement.

Movement means change and so time begins.

There is a past, a present and a future.

Love now flows.

Manifestation begins and Love is ultimately received.

# Table of Contents

# Everything Starts at the End of the Journey

Before any one thing, before time itself, before any limit or edge there is simply **Love**, there is oneness. Somehow, beyond comprehension or understanding, this pure **Unity** of *Love* through **Grace** creates duality which comes into being as *Love* flowing in the form of **Spiritual Energy**. *Love* i s **The Source** of all and *Spiritual Energy* is *Love* in Motion. As soon as *Spiritual Energy* flows creating duality, then the illusions of movement and time arise. As *Spiritual Energy* flows its vibration slows down and crystallises creating the vast spiritual dimensions.

Within these vibrational dimensions the **Spiritual Hierarchy** of intelligence come into being. Eventually as the vibration slows down through successive dimensions then the lower dimensions of manifest creation arise. This is what you experience as the world, thoughts and feelings around and within you. Within these lower dimensions you play the dance of birth, life, and death. All very real from your perspective and yet all an illusion when

1

viewed from the higher spiritual dimensions.

This is not a belief system, imagination, or idea and the labels and descriptions given are only a guide. Knowledge and understanding is not the same as being that which is described. It is your potential, when you are vibrationally ready, to realise *Enlightenment* returning your spirit to *Unity* and to then be present and spiritually awake on every single dimension.

The opportunity to transcend the lower dimensions and to return to the source exists for those who are vibrationally ready. Do not concern yourself with judging whether or not you are ready because if the opportunity has presented itself to you then it means you are. In reality no one is "ready" or "deserving", and spirituality is never "earned" or "achieved". Spiritual awakening and growth is the result of pure kindness which comes from *Love* via *Grace*. If you are open minded and kind of heart then that is all that is needed to start your journey.

# The Hierarchy of Intelligence and Love

Everything comes from *Love*, *The Source*, which some refer to as "*God*", "*God State*", or "*Unity*". Everything below *The Source* is simply energy vibrations emanating from *Grace*. Between *Grace,* which is the highest vibration, and the creation you experience which is the slowest vibration, consciousness and awareness give rise to spiritual intelligence organised into a hierarchy known as the ***Spiritual Hierarchy***. Within this *Spiritual Hierarchy* there exist intelligent entities in the forms of ascended souls and beings of light and energy.

Below are listed some of the main spiritual entities and beings as well as those of the lower dimensions. They are listed with those of the highest vibration first.

## *God*:

*The Source, Love, Unity,* the cause of all. Eternal, beyond vibration, beyond time, limitless, without edges. *God* has nothing to do with the idea of god as found within any religion. *God* is limitless and cannot be contained within a personality or gender. *God State* was not created and hence can never end as it is beyond time. *God* does not act, judge or punish, has no desire or needs. It is the state of *Enlightenment*, it is unconditional *Love*.

## Grace:

The channel between unity and duality allowing *Love* to flow from *The Source* into duality. *Love* enters the vortex of *Grace* and becomes spiritual energy within duality.

## Love:

The highest spiritual principle which is pure potential. *Love* flows via *Grace* into duality permeating and binding all things on all levels. It is the divine potential. As *Love* flows it manifests as spiritual energy.

## Master Principle:

The intelligence which guides the spirit back to *The Source*. The *Master Principle* is ever present and provides the potential for a spiritual journey. At times a living person may be chosen by the

*Ascended Masters* to "take on the mantle of the *Master Principle*" which means that person becomes a living **Master**, *an instrument of the Master Principle.* Being present on the physical plane a *Master* is then able to guide people back to *Enlightenment* by connecting them to **Light and Sound Energy** which is an aspect of the *Master Principle.* This process of connecting a person to *Light and Sound Energy* is known as **initiation**.

Whether you are initiated by a living *Master* or by someone who having been connected is able to work with *Divine Intelligence* directly, it is the *Master Principle* which ultimately guides the spirit back to *The Source.* The *Master Principle* creates spiritual **Light and Sound Energy** which, when you meditate upon it, guides your spirit back to *The Source.*

## *Spiritual Hierarchy*

There are 4 spiritual dimensions which are numbered from 4 to 8.

Within the 6$^{th}$ and 7$^{th}$ Dimensions there are many spiritual beings working as a collective known as the *Spiritual Hierarchy*. This term *"Spiritual Hierarchy"* is the collective name for the *Divine Intelligence* on the 7$^{th}$ Dimension that govern all things, and the *Spiritual Beings* and *Angels* of the 6$^{th}$ Dimension who act as their agents.

# The Spiritual Hierarchy

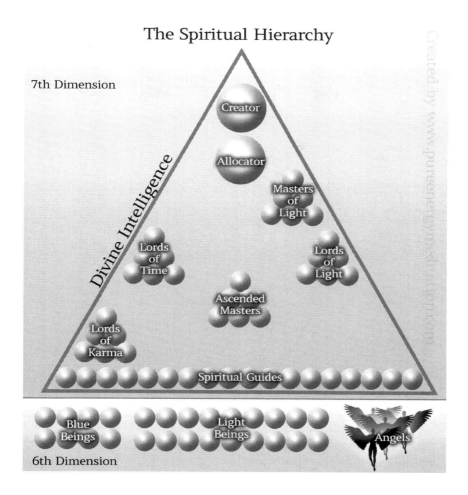

**Diagram 1.** The *Spiritual Hierarchy*. This diagram shows the different entities within the *Spiritual Hierarchy*. Where there is more than one they are shown as groups of spheres. Simple grey spheres have been chosen to represent entities to avoid confusion of colour or geometry, or to create ideas and imagination. The number of spheres shown is not important but they convey the idea that we are many and collectively "we are one".

### *Divine Intelligence*:

The highest spiritual awareness within the 7<sup>th</sup> Dimension. *Divine Intelligence* is the collective sum of different spiritual beings that together create, manage, and organise the lower dimensions. "We are one" and at the same time we, *Divine Intelligence,* consists of a hierarchy of beings including *Creator, Allocator, Masters of Light, Lords of Light, Lords of Time, Ascended Masters, Lords of Karma,* and *Spirit Guides*.

### *Creator:*

That which creates everything including universes, plants, flora, fauna, souls and mankind, and oversees their entire cycle of life to death. The creator exists within duality and is not found within *Unity*.

### *Allocator:*

Allocates the divine spark of spirit for each life and death including that of humans.

## Masters of Light:

They direct the flow of spiritual light and work with the *Master Principle* communicating between the hierarchy of beings within *Divine Intelligence* and the *Master Principle*.

## Lords of Light:

The *Lords of Light* send the waves of spiritual energy known as the *Light Wave*, which contain the potential to allow those already connected to the *Light and Sound Energy* to make the expansions into higher dimensions and to eventually realise *Enlightenment*. This *Light Wave* is channeled from *The Source* via *Grace*. Thus the *Lords of Light* provide the opportunity for a spiritual journey to progress. The *Light and Sound Energy* which the *Light Wave* reveals is one manifestation of the *Master Principle*. They are also known as the *Lords of Initiation* as they provide the opportunity for you to receive first initiation and thus start your spiritual journey.

## Lords of Time:

They manage the timing and order of events on lower levels. The illusion of free will within the lower dimensions means that events which are scheduled by the *Lords of Time* may not happen as designed on the higher dimensions.

## Ascended Masters:

Ascended Masters oversee and guide those who are intended to become living *Masters* or those souls who will become *Ascended Masters* upon the death of their person. When a person's soul is vibrationally ready then the *Lords of Karma* recommend them to the *Ascended Masters*. If the *Ascended Masters* agree that the soul is ready then an *Ascended Master* will take over the role of guiding that person and so replace their normal *Spirit Guide*. In rare cases one *Ascended Master* may guide two individuals at the same time, for example if a living *Master* is coming to their end and a new *Master* is to be trained. In such a case the same *Ascended Master* may be guiding both people. Generally it is one *Guide* per person though.

*Ascended Masters* can choose to incarnate again using the same soul as before if there is work to be done. They will not necessarily have an *Ascended Master* as their guide and will not automatically remember that they are an Ascended Master. The *Ascended Master* who incarnates will have a life purpose to help guide humanity.

## Lords of Karma:

They manage **Karma** and allocate each person their individual *Spirit Guide*. They also assess the work of *Spirit Guides*. They oversee the training of the soul to evolve through experience and learning. Collaborating with *Ascended Masters* they select the incarnations for each soul.

## Spirit Guides:

These are souls of people who have died and then are chosen by *Ascended Masters* to remain in the higher dimensions to act as guides for other souls who are going to incarnate. They are assigned a person to guide by the *Lords of Karma*. These *Spirit Guides* are souls who in their previous life raised their vibration through a life aligned with *Love* or via a spiritual journey. Not all *Spirit Guides* had attained *Enlightenment* though some had, all however were pure of intent and had a desire for deeper spirituality. Before being assigned to act as a *Spirit Guide* for a soul which is going to incarnate, a *Spirit Guide* is first given training from senior *Spirit Guides*.

Once the person a *Spirit Guide* has been assigned to has died and their soul has let go of the mind and emotions then the work of the *Spirit Guide* is complete. The *Spirit Guide's* work is then appraised by the *Lords of Karma* who then allocate the next person to be guided. The process of learning and raising their vibration towards *Love* continues for *Spirit Guides* as it does for your soul too.

## Light Beings:

These are allocated by *Ascended Masters* to help souls who incarnate. You have a *Light Being* assigned to you before birth. Before assignment to you the *Light Beings* first observe and learn so they are ready for their role with you. The *Lords of Light* are the head of the *Light Beings* and the *Light Beings* work with you to help you learn about the *Lords of Light*. They take on the role of being your guiding conscience. The *Light Being* joined with you when you were a foetus in the womb at about 14 weeks, the same time that your soul joins. It stays with you until your death. When you listen to your *Light Being* it will always guide you in the direction of *Love*. It is trying to make you aware of the *Lords of Light,* and thus guide you back to remembering your true nature. This *Light Being* is separate from you but sits within your aura, always there. As you raise your vibration the *Light Being* has its vibration correspondingly raised. If you start the spiritual journey and receive initiation into *Light and Sound Energy* thus accessing higher dimensions then your *Light Being* is also taken back into these spiritual dimensions. The *Light Being* can go as far as you go within duality but unlike you cannot become *Enlightened* as it lacks a physical body and is therefore not present on all dimensions. It however does share in the your raised vibrations. It is a positive symbiotic relationship.

## Blue Beings:

These are beings of energy who were created about 2000BC by

the *Lords of Light* to help and guide humanity. There are 80 *Blue Beings* and they work in pairs. At certain times a person will be chosen to work with a *Blue Being*, in which case they merge with a *Blue Being* so that their own aura and the *Blue Being's* energy become one. These *Blue Beings* are beings of *Love* and a person who is connected to a *Blue Being* will live a life in which they aspire to heal, help others, and raise the vibration of themselves and others towards *Love*. They may not be aware that they are connected to a *Blue Being*. The *Blue Being* who is joined with a living person stays connected to their paired *Blue Being* on the higher dimension. In this way there can be up to 40 *Blue Beings* working with people at any one time. Not all of the *Blue Beings* will be present on Earth at all times. The *Blue Beings* remember the souls of those people who have hosted them in the past and they remain watchful over such souls and their future incarnations as if they are part of a family. They may revisit such a soul temporarily to help guide them, though this is rare.

*Blue Beings* may mistakenly be the idea behind "indigo children".

People have an overall hue to their aura and as the vibration of humanity is being raised due to those people meditating on *Light and Sound Energy* then the hue of people's auras is shifting towards indigo as it incorporates more of the faster vibrations.

## Angels:

These are beings who may come and protect you if you are in danger and it is not your time to die. They reside on the higher 6th Dimension but can take physical form within the 3rd Dimension if needed to intervene and protect someone. When they take on physical form they will appear as normal people, however when perceived on higher dimensions then they may appear to have wings, which is their energy shape.

There are a fixed number of *Angels* and they each have different a vibration. They do not act as *Spirit Guides* but rather to protect a person. As well as physically manifesting they may manifest as energy and stay unseen with a person for a period of time offering protection, for example from negativity. Unlike guides, which were once people with souls, *Angels* were never manifest in the same way, rather they are vibrational energy beings created by the *Creator*.

## Elementals:

Found within the 2nd Dimension, *Elementals* manage the flora and fauna in the 1st Dimension.

## Human Beings:

Humans beings are primarily located in the 3rd Dimension at this time. Unlike the creatures and plants listed below like elephants and whales, you have the potential to reconnect with the higher dimensions and attain *Enlightenment* because your aura and chakra system are complete and aligned vertically with the sun.

## Flora and Fauna:

Within the lower Dimension there exist many different vibrations and expressions of intelligence and spiritual energy crystallised into form. These can be grouped into the Animal, Vegetable and Mineral kingdoms. Below are described some of them: All are governed by the *Elementals*.

## Elephants:

Like humans they have 7 main chakras. They can be aware on higher spiritual dimensions but because they do not align their chakras with the sun and remain on 4 legs then their vibration cannot be raised enough to realise *Enlightenment*. As with all animals, they cannot be initiated but they are however spiritually aware, and below humans Elephants are the most spiritual of animals on our planet at this time.

## Whales:

Although they cannot attain *Enlightenment* they are sentient and spiritual. For centuries they have been channelling healing energy to humans to try and heal humanity and make people aware of the damage they do to the planet. They are an ancient race and possess 5 main chakras.

## Dolphins:

They too possess 5 main chakras and are able to be spiritually aware. They are also channelling healing.

## Land Animals:

Some possess 4 main chakras such as cattle and horses while others only have 3 chakras for example cats and dogs. Dogs and cats possess a crown chakra, heart chakra and a lower chakra which is equivalent to the solar plexus, sacral and base chakra of mankind merged into one.

## Serpents & Fish:

They do not possess a crown chakra as they draw their energy from the ground, rather than the sun.

## Sea Creatures, Birds, and Insects

These are all present within the 1$^{st}$ Dimension.

# The Dimensions

There are eight discrete dimensions found between *Grace* at the top and the slowest vibration of **Manifest Creation**. This is not to be confused with the three dimensions of left right, up down, and forwards backwards people use to describe the physical plane. These physical dimensions are mathematically represented as X, Y and Z. The eight dimensions are vibrational dimensions all existing within duality, where each is faster than the one below it. The faster the dimension the more the "intelligence" within it is aligned with *Love*. As well as the eight dualistic dimensions there is *Unity* which is referred to as the 9th Dimension, though being *Unity* it does not have a limit, vibration or form.

# 1st Dimension

This is the vibrational plane where the consciousness of all flora and fauna reside. The plants and animal kingdoms. This includes the life of the oceans and of earth. This is the slowest dimension in terms of vibration.

## 2ⁿᵈ Dimension

This is where the *Elemental* beings reside. They are the guardians of the first dimension. The mythical pixies, faeries, and so forth. Young children up to about the age of seven are much more sensitive to the vibrations of the 2ⁿᵈ Dimension and so may perceive these *Elemental* beings. Unfortunately if they do mention it to their parents then they are normally told they are imagining it or are being silly and so by the time the child has grown up they themselves dismiss these things.

## 3ʳᵈ Dimension

This is where human beings currently have their consciousness. It is also where negative thoughts, deeds, and actions express. When you express such negativity then you keep your awareness focused into the 3ʳᵈ Dimension.

## 4ᵗʰ Dimension

This is where your desire starts the process of manifesting and creating the 3ʳᵈ Dimensional world around your through your feelings.  It is the dimension of "cosmic ordering".  Contained within the 4th Dimension are the astral, mental, and higher mental planes.  The 4th Dimension is where you express kind and positive feelings raising your soul's vibration more in the direction of *Love*.  It is within this 4th Dimension that your spiritual journey begins, once you are initiated.

## 5th Dimension

This is where those desires your have cosmically ordered in the 4th Dimension are prepared for sending down to manifest into the 3rd Dimensions.  This is where wellbeing of yourself and others comes from.  How you think dictates how you feel and how you physically manifest.  The 5th Dimension is the point of manifestation into the lower dimensions, with the "Atmic Principle" being the gateway through which spiritual energy flows from the 6th Dimension into the 5th Dimension and downwards.

# 6<sup>th</sup> Dimension

This is where the *Spiritual Hierarchy* agree or not to the granting of those desires you have cosmically ordered. What is granted will depend on whether it resonates with your life-plan and karma. This is the intuitive realm. It is where *Angels* and the *Light Beings* collaborate with the *Ascended Masters* to assist and guide you.

# 7<sup>th</sup> Dimension

These are the spiritual light planes. *Divine Intelligence,* which is made up of a hierarchy of spiritual beings, is found here. These spiritual beings include the *Spirit Guides* and *Ascended Masters*. Upon 2nd initiation the meditator is granted access to the 7<sup>th</sup> and 8<sup>th</sup> Dimensions by the *Lords of Light* who are also part of the *Divine Intelligence* and the *Master Principle* found on the 8<sup>th</sup> Dimension.

# 8<sup>th</sup> Dimension

This is undifferentiated spiritual energy. The higher spiritual planes.  The *Master Principle* exists on the 8th Dimension and through the *Divine Intelligence* it allows initiated meditators to reconnect with the flow of *Love* from *The Source* and guides their spirit back to *Unity* which is *Enlightenment*.

# 9th Dimension

*Unity, The Source, God, Eternity.*   This is the state of *Enlightenment*, there is nothing beyond.  *Love* is found within the 9th Dimension and through *Grace* it flows into the lower dimensions.  *Grace* is the metaphoric doorway through which a spirit returns to *The Source* and from which *Love* flows as spiritual energy from *The Source*.  This dimension is formless, timeless, and limitless and does not exist within duality.  There is no vibration within *Unity*.

# Manifest Creation (1st to 3rd Dimensions)

As human beings you occupy the lower three dimensions in your everyday life and so dimensions 1 to 3 can really be grouped together and considered as "manifest creation".  Considering the lower three dimensions in this way makes it easier for people to understand the limits of creation and where a spiritual journey really begins. The $3^{rd}$ dimension and downwards are creation whereas spiritual awareness only starts on the $4^{th}$ Dimension.

## Spiritual Realm ($4^{th}$ to $8^{th}$ Dimensions)

Upon initiation into spiritual *Light and Sound Energy* you are given a spiritual vehicle allowing you to access the $4^{th}$, $5^{th}$ and $6^{th}$ dimensions. Further expansions guided by the *Master Principle* allow access to the $7^{th}$ and $8^{th}$ dimensions. The final expansion to attain *Enlightenment* allows your Spirit to return to the $9^{th}$ Dimension transcending the spiritual planes and everything below within duality.

ENLIGHTENMENT     9th     LOVE

GOD

UNITY

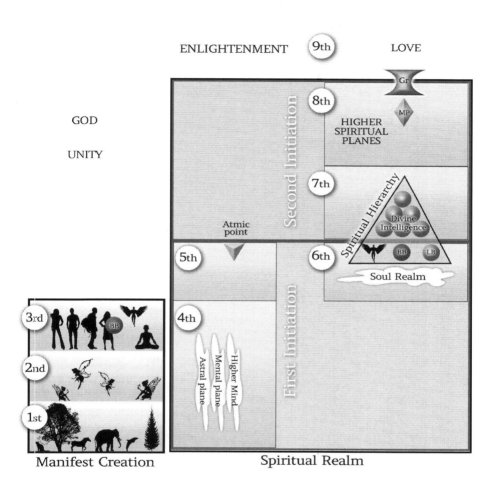

Manifest Creation          Spiritual Realm

**Diagram 2 (previous page).** The Dimensions. This diagram represents the nine dimensions with the 9th Dimension being the space around the other eight a s *Enlightenment* is formless. The images and icons shown are only representations. For example only a few fauna and flora are shown in the 1st Dimension, but this dimension contains all flora and fauna. The use of colour has been kept to a minimum to remove any confusion as many people associate colour with chakras. The colour has been used simply to show that the scope of first initiation shown in pink is different from the scope of second initiation shown in light blue. Some of the structures within the spiritual realm are highlighted in yellow. The choice of colours is purely to make it easier to see the differences and notice the features. The chakra system with its associated colours only exists within the 3rd Dimension. Each dimension is labeled with the number in the white label.

The first three dimensions are grouped together and are found alongside the 4th Dimension. The 5th Dimension sits above the 4th. The 5th and 6th Dimensions are vibrationally separate. Above the 6th Dimension sits the 7th and 8th Dimensions. Beyond all dimensions is *Enlightenment* which has no form. It is referred to as the 9th Dimension but does not exist in duality like the other dimensions. Key to understanding the symbols: Gr = *Grace,* MP = *Master Principle,* BB = *Blue Beings*, LB = *Light Beings.*

# The Light Wave

Everything emanates from *The Source* and everything is cyclic in nature, like the changing seasons or waves coming and going on a beach.    Manifest creation, the lower three dimensions, goes through cycles of being more spiritually awake and asleep.  When creation is more asleep then it is vibrationally colder entering a spiritual winter season.  During such a time those spiritual beings closest to *The Source* of *Love,* who you may call the *"Lords of Light"* send down waves of awakening love, waves of light energy.  While the *Light Wave* is being transmitted you have the opportunity to be initiated into *Light and Sound Energy.*  Having been initiated the *Light Wave* allows you to expand your awareness further into higher spiritual dimensions thus rediscovering your true spiritual nature.   As you expand your awareness your soul vibration is also raised.   Expanding your awareness happens through meditation on the *Light and Sound Energy* which guides your awareness to explore the spiritual dimensions initiation provides access to.   Further expansions grant access into higher dimensions by the grace of the *Light Wave*.

The *Master Principle* allows your spirit to transcend the limits of the lower dimensions, re-connecting with the higher spiritual dimensions, which are themselves created by *Love* flowing, and to finally realise that you are *The Source*, *Love* itself, receiving *Enlightenment*.

Having received *Enlightenment* you can channel higher vibrations of spiritual energy into manifest creation and thus the vibration of manifest creation is raised. There can be no change without fresh energy and when you are connected to the *Light and Sound Energy* you can act as a channel for *Love* from higher dimensions to enter into the 3$^{rd}$, 2$^{nd}$ and 1$^{st}$ Dimensions. Each person who is connected to spiritual *Light and Sound Energy* is a conduit for *Love*.

This is more than just a poetic picture, idea, philosophy, or belief. It is reality and this is a time when a *Light Wave* is being directed. Each person who connects to it through a process called "initiation", has the potential if they choose to channel *Love*, spiritual light, and healing energy allowing these positive demonstrations of flowing *Love*, to express all the way into creation. The *Light and Sound Energy* provides the potential to be guided back to *The Source*.

In order to understand your role as a human being within the different dimensions it is helpful to first understand what your personality and identity is, what your life is, and also what is your soul and spirit. It is also important to understand the difference between a "soul journey" and a "spiritual journey" and to know about initiation, the process by which you may become able to start a spiritual journey.

## What is Your Soul?

Each and every person who lives has a **soul**, manifested into form to allow itself to experience choices, and thus to learn from the consequences of those choices. Learning is not just about knowledge but about changing your vibration. Prior to incarnation your soul exists on the 6th Dimension within the soul realm.

All souls are part of the overall soul realm or as it may be called the "soul essence". Some people use the analogy of a tree with many branches to describe how the soul realm is organised. Consider that the leaves of a tree are the individual souls and those leaves on the same twig being close to each other are your soul family. But then your soul is also close to and vibrationally connected to those other souls on your branch. All souls are ultimately connected as they are all part of the same soul tree.

Sometimes members of a soul family may incarnate together, again and again over different lifetimes, to share a journey and experience. You may have been friends with someone in a previous life and now in this life together you are their sibling, parent, lover, grandparent, or friend again. This is not by chance but by design, where the *Lords of Karma* give you both another opportunity to resolve karma and learn lessons together. Any changes to your soul's vibration will also affect those souls within your soul vibration, and life lessons can intertwine.

Your soul enters you when you are a foetus at 14 weeks and resides within your heart chakra. The soul will stay with your body throughout your life. Your soul may detach from your physical body several moments before death. Some time after death your mind and emotions are let go of and your soul remerges with your soul family. Having been released from the illusion of a personality created when your soul joined with the mental and emotional bodies, the soul takes the big sleep where it can forget the personality and remember its true soul nature, which was there before your personality was created.

## What is Your Spirit?

There is often confusion about what is soul and what is spirit. Spirit is the divine spark directly from *The Source*. Spirit is the energy of *Love* used to create and animate. Your spirit and soul are separate, the former being energy the latter being form. Without spirit there is no awareness or life since it is vital energy. Soul is an identity on spiritual realms and while your soul joined you at 14 weeks, your spirit only connects to you as you draw your first breath.  Spirit energy stays around your etheric body and leaves your body when you die, whereas the soul may detach from your body several moments before the death of your physical body.

# The Soul's Life Purpose

Prior to birth your spirit, working with higher beings within the *Spiritual Hierarchy* decide on the life purpose and life lessons for your soul.  The environment, birth time, astrology, location, mental body, emotional body, physical body, predispositions, strengths and weaknesses, parents, foetus, physical characteristics, and life situation are all pre-selected to provide the best chance of your soul experiencing and learning it's life lessons and purpose.  These varied factors contribute to make your personality.

The potential life-lessons and plans are varied from soul to soul, but they generally revolve around creating opportunities to raise your soul's vibration towards *Love*.  This can be through acquiring knowledge and understanding in the form of academic style learning, but also through direct life experiences as well. Life lessons present opportunities to learn those qualities like humility, kindness, gratitude, compassion, and forgiveness, which allow you to live and express more of a "life of *Love*". Each person's life lesson can be very specific for example "to learn to let go of being in control" or "to learn to listen without judging". The lessons are chosen to raise the vibration of the soul and therefore ultimately to raise the vibration of the soul family too.

## Understanding Choice and Karma

In order for your soul to raise its vibration through learning from experiences you need the illusion of **choice**. In an awakened state aligned with *Love* there can be no choice because spiritual beings aligned with *Love* already understand how all action either moves more towards unity and *Love* or more into duality. Spiritual beings which know themselves to be from *Love* always move towards balance and unity, towards *Love*. So to have the illusion of choice you need to forget that you are *Love*, and that you came from *Love*. You need to forget that there is a part of you which is spirit. So upon your soul joining to your human form you fell asleep to your true nature; you forgot you are a multi-dimensional spiritual being of *Love*. Forgetting you came from *Love* was necessary to allow you the illusion of choice and free will.

Your freedom to make choices at will can take you more towards *Love*, raising your vibration, or more away from *Love*, lowering your vibration. Your life purpose is designed to allow you to explore these choices in a specific way with the ultimate goal of raising your vibration. **Karma** can be thought of as a non-judgemental, non-moralistic way of measuring how well you are aligned with your life plan and your life lessons. If you live your life congruently with your life plan then there is no karma.

Two people who make the same choices may not have the same karmic outcome, it depends on their particular life plan and life lessons. This is why there can be no morals or judgement when it comes to karma. What is appropriate for one person's life plan may not be appropriate for another persons's. Karma is not a system of punishment as some believe. Karma is there to guide your soul's vibration towards *Love*. If you deviate away from your personal chosen life plan then karma builds and your life will develop friction and pressure, motivating you to realign with your pre-chosen life plan.

In being born you have forgotten your true nature and also your life purpose, but you are never alone. On higher dimensions you have a personal *Spirit Guide* who is with you from your first breath until your soul, having realised that the body has died has decided to let go of your mind and emotions. Your *Spirit Guide* is constantly there guiding you to stay on your life's path. *Spirit Guides* are beings who do not manifest into the lower vehicles to take on human form, but stay on the 7$^{th}$ Dimension on a higher vibration than the soul realm. Because your *Spirit Guide* already knows your life plan and purpose and is on a higher spiritual dimension aligned with *Love*, then they are able to help and guide you with clarity. Whether you are aware of them or not they are there supporting you all the time. In addition there may be times when other *Spirit Guides* come and go to help you or work with you, but your personal *Spirit Guide* is with you from the very start till the end.

# Death is Not The End

When your physical life ends and you let go of your physical body, the different parts including your mind, emotions, spirit, and soul eventually go their separate ways.

Before separating though, your mind and emotional bodies remain intact for some time after death, allowing your soul to experience a period of dreaming in which you dream a "heaven" like dream. The qualities of this dream will be determined by your beliefs, your imagination and your vibrational state.

Eventually your lower vehicles including your mind and emotional body are let go of and they break down to be recycled by other incarnating souls. This can lead to the illusion of reincarnation where one person believes they were someone else in another life. It is because an old memory or emotion which has yet to fully break down has been incorporated into the emotional or mental body being created for the newly incarnating soul to use.

A while after physical death and the dream period, your soul fully merges back into the soul essence. Upon merging your soul family is then vibrationally enriched with the vibrational consequences of the learnings your soul has experienced. When one soul is vibrationally raised the other family members are also raised. Your soul family are therefore always on a similar vibration. A soul can only raise the vibration of its soul family. If a soul returns with a lower vibration then the soul family's vibration is not lowered.

After remerging with your soul family, your soul will have a big dreamless sleep, in which your soul forgets about the life you just had.

## Your Karma Once You Have Died

If you have built up karma then that karma will be incorporated into your life lesson for the next manifestation of your soul and the karmic cycle of life continues. In this way you and your soul family are constantly evolving towards the highest vibration in the direction of *Unity* and *Love*.

## Where Does Spirit go When You Die?

On death the spirit returns to the highest vibrational level you experienced while you were alive.  If you were *Enlightened* then the spirit is already free having returned to *The Source*.

Your *Spirit Guide* returns to the guide pool and may assigned to be a guide for another soul.   The *Light Being* returns to the highest vibration within duality that you realised while you were alive.

Having attained Enlightenment your spirit is free, returning to *The* Source and with the exception of *Ascended Masters,* the soul will not manifest again within the lower dimensions.   After physical death, having attained *Enlightenment* your soul may go beyond the soul realm on the 6th Dimension and join the *Spiritual Hierarchy* on the 7th Dimension.   Souls ascending to the 7th Dimension will become *Spirit Guides* to help other souls that have yet to ascend.  The exact role your soul will fulfil is chosen by the *Spiritual Hierarchy* and your soul continues to learn and evolve on these higher spiritual planes.

# Spiritual Initiation

The process of *initiation* is the very first step on a spiritual journey as it opens the crown chakra allowing a permanent connection to be made to spiritual energy vibrations which come from the *Master Principle.* These faster spiritual vibrations are beyond the awareness of the limits which make up your personality. Being faster they cannot be perceived by your mental, emotional, etheric or physical bodies, which are sometimes referred to as your lower vehicles.

The potential for people to become initiated is cyclical in nature and is only available when the *Master Principle,* working either through the *Lords of Light* or through a living *Master,* sends a *Light Wave* of energy. These *Light Waves* are also described as "grace".

The word "initiation" is used in different contexts, and so you must be clear what a "spiritual initiation" is. A spiritual initiation can only be performed by a person who has already been initiated into spiritual energy and therefore has access to spiritual energy from the *Master Principle*.

There are a number of ways a person may receive spiritual initiation:

- Directly via a living *Master*;

- Via someone who has first been initiated by a living *Master*, realised *Enlightenment*, and then been given the ability to act as an extension of the *Master* by the *Master*;

- Via someone who, having already been initiated, has made a connection with the *Spiritual Hierarchy* and who is pure of heart and neutral so that the *Spiritual Hierarchy* can channel the initiation through them.

Because people's awareness is trapped within the 3rd Dimension then the spiritual initiation must be carried out between two people who are both alive and present on the physical plane. A person can not be initiated after death or via a being which is not physically present. During first initiation the initiator places their hands on the head of the person to be initiated. The initiator must be neutral and aligned with *Love* to allow the *Lords of Light* to overshadow them and thus connect with the person receiving grace on every level. It cannot be done remotely.

The exception is someone who is born to be a *Master* as they already have the connection to the *Master Principle*. In this way a single *Master* may initiate many others who can then go on to initiate many more acting as conduits for *Love*. From one plant many seeds can grow.

Understand that initiation is not the imparting of knowledge, belief system, postures, mandalas, symbols or geometry, affirmations, or mantras. It is not written, spoken, or based in movement. It is an energy initiation in which the receiver becomes aware of spiritual *Light and Sound Energy* on a higher vibrational level than that which they have had access to up to that moment. It is not an experience but a permanent connection.

There are three initiations that a person must have to attain *Enlightenment*. After the first initiation the meditator does not need to be physically present with their *Master* or teacher in order to receive second and third initiations.

## First Initiation

The process of first initiation into spiritual *Light and Sound Energy* provides new spiritual bodies for you to be present within the $4^{th}$, $5^{th}$, and $6^{th}$ Dimensions. Having these new vibrational bodies which correspond to the vibrations on these dimensions grants you, the meditator, potential to access the different vibrational planes within these three dimensions, starting with the $4^{th}$ Dimension. Your crown chakra is opened for the first time upon first initiation, allowing you to become aware of these new spiritual bodies beyond your lower vehicles.

## Second Initiation

Upon second initiation your spirit is granted access to the $7^{th}$ and $8^{th}$ Dimensions. You have the potential to transcend the limits of your mind and become one with all of duality, but you are still not *The Source* as your awareness is within duality and is still based on vibration.

# Third Initiation

The third initiation is transcending all limits including all vibrations to become the 9$^{th}$ Dimension, where the spirit is set free. There is nothing beyond this, this is complete and the state o f *Enlightenment* is impossible to put into words since it is something you must "be" rather than "know". It is *Love, Unity, The Source, God.*

# Fourth Initiation

A living *Master* may carry out a what is called a "fourth initiation" on someone who is *Enlightened.* Unlike the first three this "initiation" does not lead to higher vibrational awareness or further expansion, since the meditator is already *Enlightened* and hence there can be no more expansion or letting go as they are already everywhere. This fourth initiation does not reveal more, instead it creates a neutral channel within the meditators spiritual and lower vehicles including their aura. This neutral channel allows them to become a conduit for the energy transmitted by the *Master Principle.* The *Master* would then control the flow of this energy through the meditator, who effectively acts as an extension of the *Master*. The fourth initiation is not necessary since someone who has already received first initiation and who is pure of heart and able to be neutral can act as a conduit for the *Lords of Light* allowing them to initiate others. Upon *Enlightenment* it is much easier but although rare it is not impossible to do so beforehand. To initiate, especially before *Enlightenment* does require humility, neutrality and unconditional *Love* in order for the neutral channel to be present. Initiation is usually given by an *Enlightened* person.

On being given first initiation it is possible for you to spontaneously realise two or three initiations at the same time. For example when given first initiation you may spontaneously make the expansion into second initiation at the same time. There are even those who expand into *Enlightenment* having been given first initiation. This is because the *Light Wave* which allows for expansions is neutral and contains the potential for people to make the expansions. In effect the person realises first initiation and then in quick succession realises the other expansions too. The exception is the fourth initiation which is not an expansion but rather a changing of the geometries of the vehicles of the person. 4$^{th}$ initiation must be done by a *Master*. If working directly with the *Spiritual Hierarchy* then it is not necessary to receive fourth initiation in order to initiate others.

Spontaneously realising multiple state changes is rare and there are advantages and disadvantages to this happening. It is not within your control as the meditator. Each person will have a different journey and it is only ego and personality which compares yourself to others. Whenever anyone realises a state change from initiation then it is a moment for joy no matter how long it took or how quickly. Remember you are all part of a whole and when one person's spirit raises its spiritual awareness then everyone benefits. There is no room for jealousy or comparison within a life of *Love*.

The phrase "realises a state" means that the person has experienced their spirit expanding into the higher dimensions which the initiation gives access to. The personality does not become the states as the personality is a limit but it can have an experience of the spiritual expansion as the vibration of the expansion is communicated down through to the lower vehicles. This is what is meant by "realising the state". The initiation creates the potential for expansion, and the *Master Principal* guides the expansion, but you must be present and able to let go of your attachment to your personality and ego in order to realise the expansion.

## Non-Spiritual Initiations

There are teachers who "initiate" into light and sound within the lower vibrational levels but this is not a spiritual initiation. They are simply helping people become more aware of those vibrational planes (etheric, emotional, mental, higher mental, intuitive, and atmic) which they already have access to. Because they are not yet themselves connected to spiritual *Light and Sound Energy* then they cannot reveal spiritual *Light and Sound Energy*. Typically their teaching involves the revelation of some light and sound vibration which is mainly within the astral and mental planes and then the use of a mantra which again is mental in nature. They may also include the revelation of geometry and healing vibrations. There is no spiritual growth within limits, only by transcending limits, and so there is no thought or idea, mantra or geometry which can take a person beyond their own mind, since any thought or idea is itself a limit. Spiritual initiation gives access to planes of consciousness within spiritual dimensions, which you did not have access to before. These spiritual dimensions and the planes of consciousness within them vibrate at a much higher level than the body, emotions, mind, personality and even the soul. Thus a spiritual journey will take you beyond imagination, memory, ideas, visualisation, philosophy, the mind, and identity and into vast planes of energy and non-personality based awareness.

Words being limits will always fail to reveal that which is limitless and so a serious seeker of truth must find a teacher who can initiate into spiritual dimensions revealing spiritual *Light and*

*Sound Energy*.  Loyalty to a teacher is noble but only loyalty to truth leads to *Enlightenment*.  A teacher of truth does not seek aggrandisement of their ego but rather the progress of their students.  For the seeker of truth the proof is not in the words of the teacher but in the realisations and expansions which will be revealed upon being initiated by them.

Without spiritual initiation it is not possible to attain *Enlightenment* or experience the vast spiritual dimensions because your mind, emotions, and physical body are not able to vibrate fast enough to explore these faster spiritual vibrations.

It is important to understand that the state of *Enlightenment* which is "being *Unity*" and hence the cause of everything and everywhere can only be realised by a spiritual being which is simultaneously present and manifest on every single level, and on every dimension.  Thus spirit has to be present on the physical plane and all other planes to attain *Enlightenment*. Therefore you, being a spiritual being, cannot start the spiritual journey in one incarnation and then finish it in another because your body, emotions, mind, spirit, and soul separate after death. The journey to *Enlightenment* must be started and completed in one lifetime without exception.

## The Crown Chakra and Initiation

The crown chakra is one of the seven main chakras that are well known to many people at this time. Your crown chakra sits at the top of your head slightly towards the back. In some traditions it is called as the "Thousand Petal Lotus" and has 960 petals within its form. Animals also have a crown chakra but theirs have fewer petals. Through the different forms of lower vehicle meditation and exploration including mantra, kundalini, chi gong, yoga, and Reiki people can become more aware of their chakras.

With so many ideas and concepts about spirituality and meditation then the crown chakra provides a valuable point of reference for those seekers of truth who want to become spiritual. The crown chakra is at the dividing line between self exploration of the lower three dimensions and a spiritual journey into the higher dimensions and eventually beyond all limits to realise

*Enlightenment.*

Your crown chakra is the doorway to spiritual awareness and is always closed. The presence of the crown chakra though, even while closed, serves to remind you of your higher nature and to inspire you to seek out spirituality. The crown chakra is only opened by initiation into *Light and Sound Energy.* Even raising the kundalini does not open the crown chakra, rather the kundalini energy opens a smaller chakra located on top of the head in front of the crown chakra. There is not a vibration within your lower vehicles fast enough to open your crown chakra, and this is why you need initiation in order to go beyond your crown chakra. The crown chakra can only be opened from above, not from below.

The crown chakra is opened approximately 1 inch (2.5cm) diameter on first initiation and then is opened twice as large to approximately 2 inches (5 cm) upon second initiation. On *Enlightenment* it opens up twice as large again to approximately 4 inches (10cm). Once *Enlightened* a person who regularly channels light or *Love* will open the crown chakra further to about

6 inches (15cm).

A living *Master* is a channel for the *Master Principle* and so their crown chakra will be open even more once they have taken on the mantle of *Master Principle*. The next diagram shows how the crown chakra expands as a person progresses along a spiritual journey.

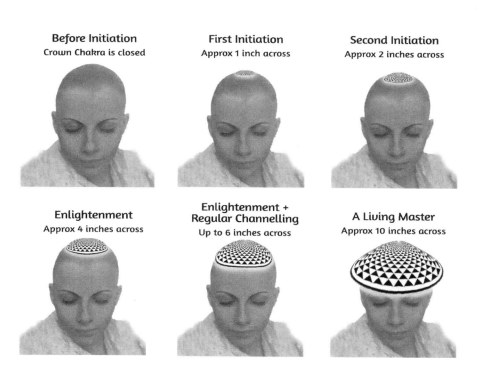

**Before Initiation**
Crown Chakra is closed

**First Initiation**
Approx 1 inch across

**Second Initiation**
Approx 2 inches across

**Enlightenment**
Approx 4 inches across

**Enlightenment +
Regular Channelling**
Up to 6 inches across

**A Living Master**
Approx 10 inches across

**Diagram 3:** The Crown Chakra. The diagram above shows how the crown chakra develops on a spiritual journey. The way the chakra is shown is for illustrative purposes only, its actual form is more detailed and varies depending

51

on if seen from below or above. The sizes are approximate but give you an idea of how it changes. Note only a living *Master* chosen by the *Ascended Masters* will take on the mantle of the *Master Principal* and have their crown chakra opened to 10 inches.

The expansion of the crown chakra is not gradual. It does not expand evenly over time. With each initiation it is opened by the *Master Principle* up to the next size corresponding to the initiation. The same is true of the different states. A person does not gradually become *Enlightened* or gradually access the second state, this is because each step is the result of an initiation and is a gift of *Grace* from the *Lords of Light* rather than earned or evolved into.

## Who can Get Initiated?

Initiation is for any human being irrespective of their gender, race, sexual orientation, colour, education, caste, religious background, or occupation. There is one recommendation which is that you must be at least 18 years of age to receive initiation. This may seem strange, but it is a suggestion from the *Spiritual Hierarchy* to remove the potential for problems created by the moral and social ideas and structures that exist within the world at this time. The age of 18 is seen by many cultures as the age of adult consent. Because initiation is such a massive step forwards in terms of a person's spiritual development, and it is not reversible, then that person must be deemed to have made the decision to progress themselves. In rare exceptions, for example if both parents are already initiated and their child is very mature in terms of life experience, then the child may be initiated, but it is recommended that the child must be at least 16 years of age, no younger. The guideline is 18 years and 16+ is only in exceptional cases.

It is human nature that having been initiated and realised *Enlightenment,* you would want to share initiation with as many people as possible. Since initiation is opening the doorway to connect with *Love,* then the desire to initiate someone is understandably borne from kindness and *Love.* The *Spiritual Hierarchy* desire for as many people as possible to get initiated and they certainly do not want to make it harder for people. The *Lords of Light* have made initiation available to the masses at this time and so an initiator does not have to ask for permission before giving initiation.

The initiator should remain respectful of the gift of being able to initiate others and if in doubt they can communicate with the *Spiritual Hierarchy* to ask for confirmation. If you do not know how to ask the *Spiritual Hierarchy* directly then there are those who are already *Enlightened* who can, and they can also teach you how to ask for yourself.

Because this is an energy initiation and the *Lords of Light* are making initiation possible planet-wide, rather than on a person by person basis then it is your responsibility as a conduit for the *Spiritual Hierarchy* to demonstrate wisdom and kindness when considering when to initiate someone. It may not always be an act of kindness to initiate someone who is still young. Always consider what is the best for the person you are helping. Sometimes a little more preparation can make a big difference.

As a person gathers life experiences they have a wealth of

emotional, mental, and intuitive resources at their disposal. They may also have matured in terms of philosophical understanding. These life resources and philosophical maturity create the lower-self structures that help the person integrate with the realisations which may come once initiated.

Without this foundation of personal resources then much of what may be revealed upon initiation and subsequent expansions into higher dimensions may be missed or dismissed by an individual who has little life experience to draw upon. Contrast is needed for realisations, and experiences provide the substrate for contrast. The same is true for someone who is older as maturity isn't solely a product of age. If someone does not have a strong foundation within their lower-self then it is harder to bring down the realisations.

Initiating a child who is young will not be a negative thing. But because regular meditation is needed in order to realise the state changes along with the ability to sit still and focus then very young children may struggle with the discipline, especially with everything that comes with developing from a child into adolescence and early adulthood. If a person does not meditate regularly on *Light and Sound Energy* then their crown chakra will close down and they will not be able to progress. The *Spiritual Hierarchy* would like people to wait till they are ideally 18 years old before being initiated as that provides them the best chance of progressing, but with this unprecedented opportunity for mass initiations they accept that human nature will lead to people being initiated at any age. The responsibility and duty of care for the initiated always rests with the initiator. There are those that have been initiated younger than 18 and that is OK. Guidelines are there to help the majority and there will always be exceptions.

## How to Prepare for Initiation

Everyone is different but there is only one *Light and Sound Energy* to which you are granted access upon initiation. The following guidelines are to help you understand how best to prepare for initiation and get the most from your meditation once you are initiated. The *Spiritual Hierarchy* want as many people to be initiated as possible and so these guidelines are not barriers. It may be that your life situation means you have very little free time, for example if you have young children. So there is flexibility, these are not hard rules. Ultimately it is up to you to be honest with yourself about how you choose to embrace a spiritual journey.

There is nothing you can do to earn the right to receive *Light and Sound Energy,* which comes from *Unity,* from *Love.* There is no action that makes you more deserving. This is because initiation is given as *Grace,* not a reward. Following the guidelines below are not to "earn" initiation, but to make sure that once you are initiated you will find an ease and joy in being able to meditate and explore the spiritual dimensions to which you will gain access.

1. Ideally you would be meditating daily for at least 1 hour but ideally 2. This may sound like a lot for a beginner, but you'd be surprised how easy it is if you start in small steps, like 15 mins and then build up to it. Once you have

access to *Light and Sound Energy* it is through regular meditation that you integrate and grow into your spiritual state of awareness. Once you are initiated you may find that time goes much faster within meditation, making it easier.

2.  A healthy lifestyle. Preferably vegetarian/vegan, alcohol free, no drugs, and not smoking. Your meditation teacher will advise you and because everyone is different and everyone's situation is different then there are some allowances. The goal is not to prevent you from moving forwards but rather to make sure you are able to get the most from your meditation. As you meditate more regularly, you may feel the urge to "clean up" your lifestyle as you become more sensitive to the subtler energies of your lower vehicles. It is possible to be initiated if you are not vegetarian, but you may struggle to progress into your meditation as the energy of eating dead animals is vibrationally very heavy. Although drugs can

create a temporary experience of the higher vibrations within the lower vehicles, they create imbalance in your aura and energy system as a result. You do not need any help to become spiritual, you just need initiation and the imbalance created from drugs will make it harder to access spiritual vibrations.

3. Being kind and loving. It is impossible to quantify this, but those who are kind and loving are the people who generally find it easiest to meditate, and to realise their states. Remember "kind and loving" includes towards yourself as well as others, after all you will have the potential to discover it is all you. You cannot seek to be one thing everywhere and at the same time not show kindness to yourself.

4. You should be able to sit and do a longer meditate. Ideally you would be practicing doing a meditate for 4 to 6 hours at least once a week. When you come to receive the energy you will typically meditate for two days of about 6

hours a day. There can be breaks within this time and once you have the energy you may find that it is a lot easier both physically and psychologically to sit for longer periods of time. In fact many people who are initiated say that they want to do longer meditates. During these meditations you have more time to explore your inner world which goes well beyond the mind and emotions and into spiritual realms founded in *Love*.

5. If you are on medication for bipolar/depression/anxiety or other psychological conditions then you must discuss this with your teacher. Equally if you have any health conditions that are neurological or affect your breathing, heart, circulation etc, then it is best to discuss this with your teacher. It does not mean that you cannot progress but your teacher needs to know so that appropriate considerations can be made.

6. How long you've been meditating is not important. People have been initiated in the past who were only

meditating for a few weeks, while others who have meditated for years. It is not about the duration but rather how easy you find it to be still, relaxed, present and accepting. Ideally you will meditate with your teacher and discuss your experience of meditation before receiving initiation.

7. There are lots of lower vehicle forms of meditation. In order to prepare for initiation you should be meditating on breath and your teacher should be able to teach you the appropriate breath meditation techniques. Sometimes mantra meditation is also used and of benefit. There are very specific mantras to assist you in getting ready for initiation and if needed your teacher will give them. Mindfulness meditation is a useful meditation philosophy but cannot take you closer to *Light and Sound Energy* meditation. It is about doing the appropriate preparation and everyone is different, so the role of your teacher is to give you the advice that is right for you.

8. Once you are initiated it is just a beginning, the advice on how much to meditate and the lifestyle recommendations also apply once you are initiated. If you stop meditating after initiation then your connection to the spiritual *Light and Sound Energy* via your crown chakra would start to close down.

## Health Considerations Before Initiation

It is also very important that you are in general good health with respect to your chakras. If you have a very blocked or imbalanced chakra then it prevents the flow of energy between the other chakras, much like a dam would block the flow of water down a river. The energy flowing from the faster chakras will build up above the blocked chakra creating more imbalance and pressure. If you have a very blocked chakra and receive initiation then you will have a lot more energy flowing through you and the imbalance of that block may then become magnified. This can result in physical symptoms. For example someone with a blocked throat chakra may experience headaches or even have their vision affected if the blocked throat chakra is not healed.

## The Development of Chakras and The Soul

Remember each soul which incarnates into a person has a life journey and is being guided. It takes about 28 years for your soul to become fully mature so that you are fully ready for your life lessons. Therefore the more time you have had to develop your soul then the more integrated you are with your life journey. This helps you to also integrate with the realisations which come from the spiritual journey. This does not mean that you must wait till 28 before being initiated, nor does it mean that at the age of 28 you are suddenly more able as a meditator. It is simply important that you understand that, just as your physical body matures, so too does your soul/life experience and your chakra system.

What is most important is that you get initiated. Initiation is a massive expansion and raising of your vibrational awareness, it must be respected as a process and not treated as an isolated event or experience because it is life changing. It is not always kindness to initiate someone without first helping them to prepare and to take into consideration their age, life-experience, situation, maturity, and importantly ability to meditate.

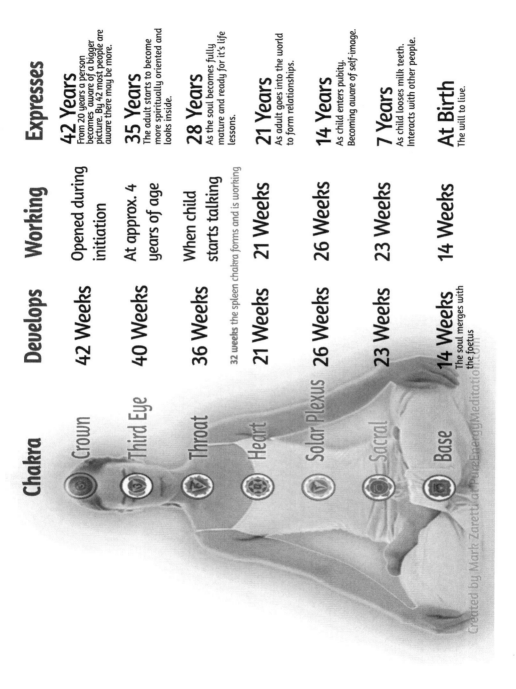

| Chakra | Develops | Working | Expresses |
|---|---|---|---|
| Crown | 42 Weeks | Opened during initiation | **42 Years** From 20 years a person becomes aware of a bigger picture. By 42 most people are aware there may be more. |
| Third Eye | 40 Weeks | At approx. 4 years of age | **35 Years** The adult starts to become more spiritually oriented and looks inside. |
| Throat | 36 Weeks | When child starts talking | **28 Years** As the soul becomes fully mature and ready for it's life lessons. |
| | 32 weeks the spleen chakra forms and is working | | |
| Heart | 21 Weeks | 21 Weeks | **21 Years** As adult goes into the world to form relationships. |
| Solar Plexus | 26 Weeks | 26 Weeks | **14 Years** As child enters puberty. Becoming aware of self-image. |
| Sacral | 23 Weeks | 23 Weeks | **7 Years** As child looses milk teeth. Interacts with other people. |
| Base | 14 Weeks The soul merges with the foetus | 14 Weeks | **At Birth** The will to live. |

Created by Mark Zaretti at PureEnergyMeditation.com

**Diagram 4 (previous page):** The Development of the Chakras. This diagram shows how the chakras develop over time measured from the start of the foetus. All the chakras are developed while the baby is within the womb, but only the lower 4 are working at birth. Each chakra has different qualities and every 7 years a person evolves to express the next chakra upwards starting with the Base chakra at birth. As each chakra is expressed the person demonstrates more of the qualities of that chakra. The effects of the crown chakra, though unopened until initiation are expressed from about 20 years but usually don't mature until about 42 years.

## Can You be *Enlightened* Without Each Step?

There is a small chance that when you are initiated you may just pass straight through to *Enlightenment*. The end goal for the *spirit* has been achieved, but because such a person did not experience each initiation as a series of steps then they lack many of the realisations and experiences within the spiritual dimensions between first initiation and *Enlightenment*. Each dimension has its own qualities and also limits and normally they are experienced as steps along a spiritual journey. Of course with subsequent meditation someone who went straight to *Enlightenment* can explore and grow into these dimensions, but they may need guidance and support.

Meditating as a first initiate is different from meditation as a second initiate, and different again when *Enlightened*. It is easier to help guide others when you have experienced the different steps yourself and someone who has gone through quickly may struggle to guide others. However the ultimate goal for the spirit has been reached when someone realises *Enlightenment*. You should not feel disheartened if you do not go straight through as there is much to learn from each of the different steps and in the majority of cases each person progresses one step at a time. Each expansion is in itself an incomprehensible leap from what the you had access to before. First initiation is vast in comparison to the lower vehicles. Second is vast in comparison to first initiation and all the dimensions fade into insignificance when contrasted to *Enlightenment*.

# The Personality is Not Enlightened

On a spiritual journey starting with first initiation and culminating in *Enlightenment* it is your spirit which is set free. The spirit is the metaphoric drop of water rejoining the ocean. The spirit is divine, it is from *Love* and can return to *The Source*. Your soul,

**67**

which exists within duality, is an identity as are your mind and body and so your soul and lower bodies do not get *Enlightened*. This is why after *Enlightenment* there are still your soul's life lessons and plan to explore while you are alive. Having been lucky enough to have had *Enlightenment* revealed your soul has more potential to raise its vibration further and faster as it has access to the vaster planes of consciousness and is now supported by the flow of *Love* from *The Source*, which now constantly flows through it. Your spirit has become *The Source*.

Even upon *Enlightenment* your personality remains hindered by the veil of manifest creation, with the mind and emotions creating the illusion of the personality and ego. Moments of clarity come in the form of realisations experienced on your spiritual journey. Understanding arises from moments of stillness, where you let go of the lower vehicles and connect with the higher aspects that are now accessible in meditation through practice. But even when *Enlightened* you will not fully understand what you are while you are still alive. It is because your experience is being filtered through the limited vehicles of your soul, mind, and emotions.

The *Spiritual Hierarchy* however, being ever present on higher dimensions have total clarity as they are not limited by a mind or emotions and hence have no ego. Free of the illusion of manifest creation they are available to guide you on your spiritual journey, even when you have realised their true nature and attained *Enlightenment*.

The *Spiritual Hierarchy* understand better than people that *Enlightenment* is not an end but rather a beginning. Many of the *Spiritual Hierarchy* were once like you, souls who manifested and walked life's paths and also the path of a spiritual journey. Having lived a life of *Love* they now guide others to strive for the same. *Enlightenment* is the end of a spiritual journey and if you choose can be the start of a life of *Love*. There is much purpose for your soul after *Enlightenment*. The magnitude and enormity of the grace that makes *Enlightenment* possible will never be fully fathomed by your lower personality, because your personality is defined by limits, separation, judgement, and ego. But by striving to live a life aligned with *Love* then the personality becomes more aligned with the state of *Enlightenment* and can realise this higher purpose.

## You Still Have Choice When Enlightened

Every action your personality makes is a choice within the illusion of manifest creation where mind, emotions, and body are present. So even when *Enlightened* you can choose whether to align with your state and strive towards a life of *Love*, or to ignore it. The choice may not even be consciously made since your habits, beliefs, and predispositions persist even after *Enlightenment*. There is a saying that *Enlightenment* just magnifies the personality so if you have a "service to others" personality then you will have more potential to demonstrate "service to others". If you have a "service to self" personality then you will have more potential to be "service to self".

The personality does not get *Enlightened* and because *Enlightenment* comes from *Grace* and is not earned or a reward then any personality which dedicates the time to meditation and can let go with ease has the potential to be initiated and to realise *Enlightenment*. Absolute *Love* does not judge or discriminate and absolute *Grace* is available to all.

With the amazing expansions which come from the spiritual journey there are plenty of realisations and perspective to guide you to aspire towards a life of *Love*. But even *Enlightenment* does not force it. This is because you personality is not *Enlightened* and your personality from the perspective of *Enlightenment* is just a part of the whole, and is already perfect.

Prior to being born your soul manifested into creation so that you could experience and learn, and after *Enlightenment* your life lessons remain for your soul. *Enlightenment* sets the spirit free returning it to *Unity*, but the soul is still present within duality.

# Very Important: Babies and Pregnant Women

There are very important considerations when it comes to initiating pregnant women and also when physically holding babies. In order to understand why you first need to remember that the physical body is organised by the aura and animated via the chakra system.

The development of a baby in the womb is coordinated by the subtler etheric energy body which acts like a blueprint for the developing physical body. During this developmental period the baby's energy system is very fragile.

When a person is initiated their crown chakra is opened for the first time and as a result an amazing amount of energy enters their energy system, chakras, and meridians. Their kundalini will raise and there will be changes in their chakras which may speed up.

## The Risk of Miscarriage

If a woman is pregnant with a foetus which is less than 14 weeks old, then the foetus will not have yet joined with its soul. The changes to the energy of the pregnant woman during initiation may cause that pre-soul foetus to miscarriage.

It is important to understand that all structures within duality, including a baby's aura, chakras, and body require a certain amount of imbalance in order to exist and function. Everything can be considered as being a mix of yin and yang energies. If yin and yang are perfectly balanced then they cancel each other out. So any "thing" must be slightly more yin or yang in order to exist within duality.

The spiritual energy revealed during initiation is powerfully neutral and at the point of initiation imbalances are resolved in the lower vibrational vehicles of the mother. Prior to 14 weeks the foetus does not have a soul and so is unable to maintain its own energy integrity. The basic energy field of the foetus is interrupted by the neutrality created by spiritual energy of initiation causing its functioning to stop. The foetus prior to 14 weeks is unable to sustain the delicate connection between its physical body and its fragile aura. Once the soul has joined with the foetus the soul helps to strengthen the connection between the subtler energy vehicles and the developing physical body.

For this reason if a woman is pregnant or even suspects she is pregnant it is absolutely important that she does not receive initiation within the first 14 weeks. It is safest to wait until after the baby is born.

It is a very delicate subject to discuss but it is important that you understand the nature of the soul and how the soul interacts with the body. There are sometimes cases when a soul does not enter into a developing foetus because the timing is not right and the foetus without a soul attached will miscarriage. A foetus cannot be sustained without the soul forming a connection. In the future when the situation is better from the soul's perspective, then that soul enters a new foetus developing within its mother to be born into the world. It was not the right time or situation the first time but that soul is eventually born to the mother that was chosen for it. Each foetus before 14 weeks represents the potential for a soul to join and manifest into creation.

## When a Pregnant Woman Realises Enlightenment

If the developing baby in the womb is is more than 26 weeks into development and the mother realises her *Enlightenment* then the baby will also realise its *Enlightenment*. When born the baby will naturally not be capable of meditation and subsequently their crown chakra will close down. Their spirit will still be free but the personality of the baby as they grow up may be unaware that they have realised *Enlightenment*.

## The Potential in your Touch

Once you have realised your *Enlightenment* your energy system has changed considerably. When you are neutral and open hearted then you will have the potential to pass energy on to anyone you touch. There are specific points on a person's head which when you touch with your hands may make the connection and initiate them whether you consciously intend to do so or not. There are cases of people accidentally initiating people.

When holding a small baby in your hands you could accidentally make this connection and pass energy onto the baby. Even if you do not accidentally initiate the person you will be passing on a lot of energy which naturally flows from your hands as a spiritual person.

For the first three to six months of a new born baby's life there exists a small chakra on the top of their head which if over-stimulated will interfere with the functioning of their pineal gland. If this happens then the baby will become agitated, will sleep less, and may have its health affected. This chakra closes naturally between three to six months and stays closed until about 21 years of age. It reopens as they become more centred in their heart chakra at about 21 years old.

The new born babies of all mammals have this chakra open at birth as it triggers the instinct in the child to seek out its mother for protection, milk, and warmth.

It is a totally natural thing to hold a baby but if you have already been initiated and especially when you are *Enlightened* then you must be careful where you place your hands on another person. This need to take care is paramount if they are a baby of less than three months old or a woman who may be pregnant.

It is safer to use your left hand if touching a baby or person's head and to try to avoid making contact with the tips of your fingers. To have received initiation is a gift which comes with responsibility. Your touch now carries amazing potential and you must be respectful of the energy of other people as you interact with them. As you read on you will learn how this amazing energy potential can also be used to channel pure *Love*, healing, and light.

# Integration, the Art of Growing Into Your State

With each initiation the *Master Principle* allows you access to higher spiritual dimensions, without which you could never access them. Each initiation is a state change, raising your vibration. Initiations are absolute *Grace* in action, the highest demonstration of universal kindness. How much you can then be present within these spiritual dimensions depends on how well you can let go of your attachment to your lower vehicles to become more present within your spiritual vehicles on these higher dimensions. Attachment to the lower vehicles is based on habit, fear, and ego.

*Love* in the form of energy flows both ways with the *Master Principle* working to elevate your spirit back to *The Source,* and *Love* in the form of spiritual energy flowing back down from *The Source* and through your vehicles on every dimension. It is when you fully let go to the flow of energy that you experience the true magic of a spiritual journey. Ultimately setting your spirit free and in the process becoming a conduit for *Love* is the purpose of the spiritual journey to realise the state of *Enlightenment.*

Learning how to let go of your attachment to your lower vehicles, mind, emotions, and body is the key to progressing on a spiritual journey. But striving to live a life of *Love* is the way to making the most of it once you have attained *Enlightenment.*

## How Ego Holds You Back

*Love* is the cause of everything and duality creates the surfaces onto which the flow of *Love* as spiritual energy can be experienced. This spiritual energy slows down and eventually crystallises to form the manifest creation people experience in everyday life.

Your spirit is *Love* in essence and your soul when incarnated with a mind, emotions, and body create your personality from which your ego arises. The ego is the shadow cast by the limits and blocks to the flow of *Love* present within your lower vehicles. Some people call it the "little self". The ego obstructs the light of *Love* from flowing down from *The Source* through you, thus casting a shadow into creation. The more you align your personality with *Love* and thus diminish your ego then the more light and *Love* you allow to shine through you and into creation. In doing so you will find more *Love* within creation, which is the reflection of your true nature. When you allow *Love* to flow unhindered then not only do you benefit but the whole of creation benefits.

*Love*, *The Source* of all, is beyond vibration and from it through *Grace* the spiritual vibrations of light and energy, leading to change emanate. Each person who is initiated into the *Light and*

*Sound Energy* can, through humility and being open hearted, act as a channel for spiritual energy flowing from *Love*. By channelling it they are the ones raising the vibration of human consciousness and also their soul families. But even before receiving initiation a person can practice aligning with *Love* and those who do so will benefit more fully upon initiation. Aligning with *Love* benefits the soul's life journey and also the spiritual journey, because the humility and openness which stem from *Love* will make it easier to let go and make amazing realisations once initiated.

# Seekers of Truth and a Spiritual Journey

Every soul which has incarnated is on a personal journey to raise their vibration through experience and learning, and then upon physical death, remerge with their soul family to incorporate their vibration into the pool of souls, the soul realm. This soul-life cycle is perpetual and even a soul which has reached the highest vibration possible within the soul realm is not *Enlightened*, but they will be more receptive to a spiritual journey as they are at a vibrational level closer to *Love*.

Think of all dimensions and the planes within them as on a spiral. The base of the spiral is the lowest vibration and the top of the spiral is the highest vibration, beyond which is *The Source*, pure *Love*. Every soul who has incarnated into manifest creation is somewhere on this vibrational spiral. If you are following your soul's life lessons and purpose then you are moving vibrationally upwards along the spiral. If you are not aligned to your life's lessons then you may just stay still on the spiral or you may even move backwards down along the spiral, lowering your vibration. There is no judgement, souls are not labeled as good or bad, it is simply about vibration, being more aligned with *Love* or less aligned with *Love*. There is not a soul sent to manifest which starts out as negative, but personalities can become negative if their environment nurtures those negative vibrations. Negativity can be thought of as the personality getting in the way of the soul remembering its spiritual nature. Every soul starts as a positive vibration aspiring towards *Love* since *Love* is the cause of everything.

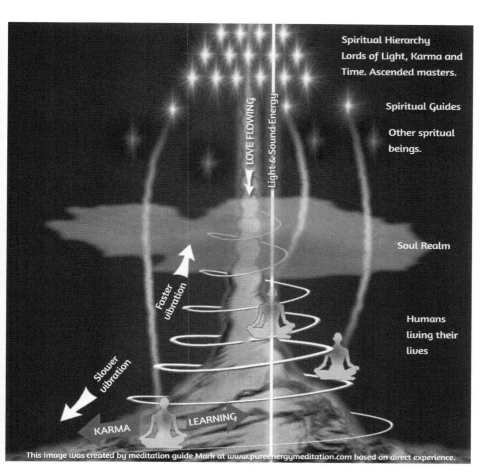

The following labels appear within the diagram:

Spiritual Hierarchy
Lords of Light, Karma and
Time. Ascended masters.

Spiritual Guides

Other spritual
beings.

LOVE FLOWING

Light & Sound Energy

Soul Realm

Humans
living their
lives

Faster
vibration

Slower
vibration

KARMA

LEARNING

This Image was created by meditation guide Mark at www.pureenergymeditation.com based on direct experience.

**Diagram 5:** The Vibrational Spiral of Souls. This metaphorically shows how souls evolve from lower vibrations to higher vibrations and how learning elevates the vibration of the soul. When a soul is not aligned to their life plan and lessons then the soul builds up karma. Karma is non-judgemental and it is not punishment. Shown also are connections between each person and their *Spirit Guides*, which are *Divine Intelligence*.

83

If, through the choices you make, you slide down the spiral, moving away from *Love*, your karma builds up to create pressure to move you back up in the direction towards *Love*. As you learn your life's lessons your vibration raises. While you are on your life plan you will not accrue karma for any actions. It is the illusion of free will which allows for choices which may take you away from your life lessons and thus build up karma.

Irrespective of the raising of your soul vibration, your soul is still a limit and cannot become *Enlightened* as a limit can never contain the limitless. It is your spirit which returns to *The Source* upon *Enlightenment* and it is the *Master Principle* which makes this possible. Your soul evolves over many incarnations moving up the vibrational spiral until it reaches a certain vibrational threshold. At that threshold then your soul may have within its life plan the potential to seek out a spiritual teacher and to become initiated, thus starting a spiritual journey.

It is possible for someone to be initiated even if it is not within their life plan, which could happen if someone else's enthusiasm to initiate them is strong enough. In such a case though the person who is initiated is unlikely to progress as they are not vibrationally aligned or ready, and it was not part of their life plan for this incarnation.

## When Does a Soul Seek Out a Spiritual Journey?

Only those who are vibrationally "ready" and have the potential pre-written into their life plan will respond to spiritual teachings and take up the call. Others may believe in spirituality, or like the philosophy and romantic ideal of spirituality but they will not move beyond belief and imagination even if the opportunity for initiation presents itself. But even some of those who are born with the potential may ignore it, because there is always the illusion of choice. If they ignore the opportunity then they may not get another chance for many incarnations, if at all. This is not a punishment, it is simply that the *Light Wave* that makes a spiritual journey possible comes and goes and so there may be lifetimes before the opportunity comes again. If their life plan was to get initiated and they turn their back on that life plan then they will accrue karma and that karma will need to be resolved before they are ready again for the opportunity.

Every soul matters without judgement or exception, and every person is a soul on the metaphoric vibrational spiral. Everyone has the potential to move further up or further down this vibrational spiral. Never judge another soul for where you perceive them to be, instead guide them if you must. Your responsibility is ultimately towards your own vibration, you cannot push or drag another soul up the spiral. But by raising your own vibration you help those near to you.

Remember the purpose of life is to explore the vibrational consequences of the choices you make and even when you are initiated and on a spiritual path you still have a soul, personality, and ego and can move vibrationally down as well as up. You must always strive to stay spiritually awake and to be aware of the vibrational consequences of your choices and actions. Aim to live a life of *Love*.

You may feel that it is unfair that some people may not get the opportunity to start their spiritual journey in their current lifetime. It is compassion and kindness to want others to know the truth. When you identify with the lower dimensions then you will naturally feel emotional and sadness towards those who may not become spiritual in this life.

As you become more aware on a higher vibrations, and practice sitting within them, for example from within the dimension where the soul essence is, then you can have realisations and understand that any one lifetime is but one of many for a soul, and that the purpose for each lifetime is to allow the soul to evolve. The soul incarnates over many different lifetimes to experience and learn, with the purpose of raising its vibration towards *Love*. As a soul learns and evolves it will raise its vibration until it is ready for a spiritual journey.

Each life has a plan and if someone does not have the opportunity for the spiritual journey in their particular lifetime then it simply means that it was not the plan of that lifetime. It is not a judgement or punishment and when you embrace unconditional *Love* then there is no room for judgement of the life plans of other souls. To think or feel sad about another person not being ready to start a spiritual journey is to judge the wisdom of the *Spiritual Hierarchy* who decided on that person's soul life plan and life lessons.

Each soul is constantly learning in order to raise its vibration and when it is ready then, when the time is right, it will have the opportunity to start on its spiritual journey. In the same way this may be your time for spirituality, and yet in previous incarnations for your soul, your soul was not ready. Had your soul been denied the lessons and experiences it's had with these previous lives, then you would not be ready at this time.

Only your own journey is under your control and as you expand spiritually you will begin to realise through experience and realisations that everything is connected and you are a part of a whole. Just as a tree in the garden doesn't mourn the loss of a leaf, because the tree understands that the cycle of leaves coming to receive sunlight and going to survive winter allow the tree to grow and thrive. Through the realisations which come with *Light and Sound Meditation* you can come to understand that each life is special and is supported by the flow of *Love* as spiritual energy. Everything is exactly as it needs to be and every person has a soul which itself is part of something much bigger. When you are that which is bigger it becomes easier to understand what life is and to have more compassion and kindness for life. It is kindness of the person to want everyone else to discover spirituality. It is kindness of the soul and a demonstration of unconditional *Love* to not judge another person's situation and to accept that there is a process each soul must go through and a reason for each incarnation.

Each person is living the life they were given in order to raise their vibration, and your own life is the only one you are responsible for. In pursuing spirituality you will also help support all those near to you too because raising your own vibration will help raise theirs. The greatest kindness you can demonstrate is to realise your own *Enlightenment*, and then to live a life aligned with *Love*. You will naturally attract those who are ready for you to help, and the whole of creation will benefit from the *Love* and light you can now channel down. You cannot force someone who is not ready to become spiritual but you can realise your own divinity and that will help them in their next incarnation as everyone is vibrationally connected.

# Are Soul Journeys and Spiritual Journeys Different?

## The Soul Journey

The journey of your soul and hence your personality through which it manifests, is an opportunity to raise the vibration of your soul through learnings experienced within manifest creation. With each carefully planned incarnation into physical life providing you new lessons. Because of free will you may drift away from your pre-chosen life purpose. However your *Spirit Guide* and *Light Being* help you to follow your life purpose and plan. You also have feelings which are giving you feedback.

When you feel joy it is because what you are doing is opening your heart chakra.

## The Spiritual Journey

The journey of the spirit is to expand awareness in order to be present on all vibrational dimensions and to finally transcend all limits upon attaining *Enlightenment* thus returning the spirit to *The Source* which is *Love*. This process starts with initiation into spiritual *Light and Sound Energy*. Subsequent meditation on this *Light and Sound Energy,* along with further initiations from the *Lords of Light* working with the *Master Principle* guide the spirit back to *The Source*.

## Does Reincarnation of the Soul Lead to Enlightenment?

No number of life incarnations of your soul can lead to *Enlightenment* without initiation since it is not your soul which is *Enlightened*. After many incarnations however your soul can reach a vibrational level where there are no more lessons to experience and thus no more karma to resolve. At this point your soul is as far up the vibrational spiral as possible, but this does not automatically lead to your *Enlightenment*. Your soul has reached the highest vibration, aligning closely with *Love* but is still separate from *The Source* which is *Unity*, because your soul is always located within duality.

Your soul-life journey explores duality whereas your spiritual journey returns your spirit to *Unity*. Think of it as each life incarnation is a single breath taken by the soul to which spirit brings the spark of life. This lifetime is one of many and as your soul evolves it may reach a point where a spiritual journey is possible allowing your spirit to escape duality and return to *Unity*.

Your soul journey exists over many lifetimes whereas your spiritual journey must be started and finished within a single lifetime.

# Enlightenment and Karma

Upon *Enlightenment* your spirit is freed from duality and has returned to *The Source,* to *Unity*. Being now present everywhere a s *The Source* is the cause of everything then your spirit still supports you. Your soul at that moment has all its karma removed and is now free of the karmic cycle of perpetual birth and death. Having attained *Enlightenment* while you are still alive you have a direct connection to *The Source* which is now your spirit. You no longer build up karma in the same way as you did before *Enlightenment*. Once Enlightened if you stay open and aligned with *Love* then since you now contain the *Lords of Karma* then your greater spiritual self will bring to your attention the karma you accrue so that it can be resolved consciously. Once *Enlightened* you have the potential to experience much more direct feedback on your choices and actions in relation to your soul's life plan. There will not be another incarnation in which to process karma you build up, instead once *Enlightened* any karma you may have at death determines the role your soul will play, and the service you will do as your soul ascends to the 7th Dimension.

As karmic feedback is experienced within duality then how well you notice and respond to karma depends on how well you choose to be receptive and present. *Enlightenment* does not automatically make you receptive but rather gives you more potential to be so. If you wish to integrate more fully with your state of *Enlightenment* then being receptive must be developed and not be taken for granted.

# The Different Kinds of Meditation

There are many meditative practices which are based on using your mind, emotions, or body. These include kundalini, mantra, mandala, yoga, Tai Chi, Chi Gong, lower light & sound, astral projection, Reiki, mediumship, affirmation, visualisation, sound bathing, crystals, chakra, colour, chanting, and many other practices. They are all based within your lower vehicles and are limited to the vibrations within your physical body, etheric web, astral body, mental bodies, intuitive awareness, and atmic vibrations.

These practices help your personality align more with *Love*. They may also help raise your soul's vibration along the metaphoric vibrational spiral of soul evolution, since being more centred and aware can help follow your life lessons and plan. However none of these practices can take you beyond the limits of the vehicles which you are using for meditation. Your mind can not be aware of anything beyond your mind. Your emotional body can not be aware of anything beyond emotions. Your physical body can not be aware of anything beyond the physical world. Only a spiritual body can be aware of spiritual energy.

Some people force themselves to have experiences using drugs such as LSD. These experiences are also limited to the lower vehicles and can only reveal vibrational awareness within your lower vehicles. They cannot open your crown chakra.

Of course experiences within the lower vehicles can be amazing when compared to normal awareness, but these experiences are much smaller than the spiritual expansion as made possible by spiritual initiation. They also do not allow for channelling of spiritual energy and so only work with the energy you already have available.

There is some value in these natural practices of meditation within the lower vehicles since they can help remove energy blocks and imbalances within the lower vehicles. By becoming more balanced you allow energy to flow with ease. As such they can be a great way of preparing for initiation, however it is important if you are serious about seeking the truth that you understand that in order to become aware and present on spiritual planes of consciousness you must be initiated into spiritual *Light and Sound Energy.*

Initiation opens the crown chakra and provides a spiritual vehicle on spiritual realms from where you can become aware of spiritual *Light and Sound Energy* coming from *The Source* and provided by the *Master Principle*. Meditation on *Light and Sound Energy* guides your spirit back to *The Source*. It is of note that the crown chakra is present but dormant and remains closed until initiation. Even practices like raising the kundalini, which raise a persons yin and yang energy currents, often referred to as serpent energy, only awakens the energy centres up to the crown chakra. Raising the Kundalini does not open the crown chakra to the higher vibrations of spiritual *Light and Sound Energy* and thus true spirituality.

Many of these practices can be very helpful for supporting you once you have been initiated. For example if you have physical discomfort when sitting for meditation then yoga and Tai Chi may help relieve the physical imbalance thus allowing you to more easily let go of your physical body awareness, going deeper into *Light and Sound Energy*. Yoga and Tai Chi also help people to find balance and harmony within their chakra and meridian systems which can also help meditators to more easily let go. In rare cases when a person is first initiated they may experience a lot of kundalini energy movement and find themselves spontaneously adjusting their body posture during meditation to realign their lower vehicles. This will pass and it shows how closely entwined energy and your physical posture are. However without initiation no movement or posture will reveal spiritual Light and Sound Energy beyond the crown chakra. The tragedy is when a person who wants to know the highest truth becomes more attached to the form of meditation they do rather than the outcome of that meditation. There are many who consider themselves "spiritual" and their hearts are open and their intention is genuine. Some are extremely experienced within the lower vehicles having dedicating years of practice to yoga, mantra, kundalini or other forms of meditation. But they have not taken the first steps on a spiritual journey and been initiated. At this time the potential to be initiated is real for any seeker of truth. There are many who have attained *Enlightenment* in a short time compared to others who have dedicated years to meditation forms within the lower vehicle, but have not transcended the limits of their lower vehicles.  Spiritual realisation is not about time, it is about energy.  Only spiritual energy can reveal spiritual truth.

# Beware the Illusion of Spiritual Awareness

Every level of consciousness, from the fastest to the slowest including the mental, astral, etheric and physical planes demonstrate the same fundamental principles which exist in duality such as location, movement, and time.  Although their qualities may be different on each vibrational level their essence none the less exists.  For example time exists on the astral plane and the physical plane but it is a lot faster in the astral plane than the physical plane.  This difference in vibrational expression leads to the adage *"as above, so below"* which means that what you experience on the physical plane is a slower vibrational expression of the same principle on a higher plane.  This varied expressing runs through all dimensions and can lead to people who experience light and sound vibration on the astral or mental planes thinking they have experienced spiritual *Light and Sound*

*Energy* which exists on a much higher spiritual dimension. Astral light is a higher vibration than physical light and so by comparison seems more amazing. Someone observing astral or mental light in meditation may think "wow I am seeing spiritual light", and although by comparison to physical light it is so much more amazing, it is not to be confused with actual spiritual light. The same is true of sound vibrations which exist on every single level. Spiritual sound vibration is not the same as sound vibrations people may experience within the lower vibrations.

Similarly before initiation it is possible for a person to experience a sense of being at one with all things, a feeling of connectedness and oneness. Such an experience may lead them to believe they are *Enlightened* because they have had an experience of "unity". However although it is an amazing and valid experience it is still within limits, they have not become *Unity*, they have experienced its lower vibrational expression within the lower planes, because the principle of Unity is found throughout every dimension. They have experienced a merging with the atmic point, the highest point within the lower vehicles. This atmic point is the point at which all manifest creation comes into being and so merging with it makes the person feel as if they are *The Source*. It is amazing and inspiring, but experiencing oneness with all things is not the same as being *Unity* which is the cause of all things.

This may seem just about semantics, the choice of words, and as such it demonstrates how words will always fail to explain higher dimensions and spiritual realisations. Words are limits and can never define the limitless. It is important that the seeker of truth not rest upon any experience no matter how amazing. All experiences require duality, with something to have the experience separate from that which they are experiencing. All experiences are within duality and hence are not *Unity*. *Enlightenment* is not an experience.

Several times people who already believe they have completed their journeys and attained *Enlightenment* have then been initiated into spiritual *Light and Sound Energy*. Each time they realise, after being initiated, that what they had previously thought of as

*Enlightenment* was a smaller expansion compared to what they now have access to. This is shared to serve to remind anyone who is a seeker of truth to strive to go beyond experiences.

A sincere seeker of truth will be guided towards a teacher who can reveal spiritual *Light and Sound Energy*. When the student is ready they will find their teacher since intention directs energy.

Remember you only have one life in which to realise *Enlightenment* since the spiritual journey must be started and completed within one lifetime. When the nature of the soul is confused with the nature of spirit then the idea of *Enlightenment* through reincarnation can arise, leading to spiritual apathy.

# What Happens to You After Enlightenment?

Once you are *Enlightened* you have gone beyond the eight dimensions of vibration and so beyond all vibration, your spirit is limitless. Within this state there are no edges and there is no duality as it is *Unity*. This means that once *Enlightened* your spirit and awareness have transcended everything and that includes the *Master Principle* and *Light and Sound Energy*. On *Enlightenment* your spirit and your awareness return to *The Source* and you realise *God State*. Once you stop meditating during the *Enlightenment* state change and bring your attention back then your spirit stays within *Unity* and your awareness returns into duality.

Because spirit is from *Love* and *Love* pervades everything then although your spirit has returned to *Unity* you still have spirit although now your spirit is omnipotent, without location, edges or time. Your spirit is *God*, your spirit is free. After realising *Enlightenment* it is possible in meditation for your awareness to revisit *Unity*.

You will also still be able to access all the lower dimensions however your potential is much greater. You can still meditate on *Light and Sound Energy* if you choose, as there is still much to explore within all the dimensions. The difference now is that there is no more expansion and everything you focus on is already within your state of *Unity, God State*.

Upon being *Enlightened* it is not the end, it is the real beginning. Your spirit reconnects with *The Source* and is now free. Being everywhere your spirit continues to support you and your awareness can be present on all dimensions. It is the ultimate joy and freedom, words simply can never describe this.

Your soul, upon death, will now be on a higher dimension having raised its vibration and will assume a role as chosen by the *Lords of Karma* and the *Ascended Masters*. Normally your soul will become a *Spirit Guide* working with the *Lords of Karma* to help guide other people along their life plan.

As a *Spirit Guide* you are soul vibration having shed the lower vehicles which created your personality. But in order to make communication easier for the person you are guiding, you can adopt a sense of identity. For this purpose you, as a *Spirit Guide,* can choose to use the personality and name of one of the lives you previously had. Usually it is the personality and name of the life you had when you became a *Spirit Guide*. Of course this personality is without the physical body and lower vehicles including, ether, mind, and emotions, and hence is also without ego. The identity the soul uses is the essence of their chosen personality rather than its manifestation.

An important question is "what happens to you once your spirit has realised *Enlightenment* before your physical body dies?".

Remember your personality and soul are not the part that is *Enlightened* but they will now be connected to the spirit which is fully present on all dimensions and is also beyond all limits having returned to *The Source*. This means that the personality is now able to be a channel for amazing spiritual energy vibrations coming directly from *The Source*, from *God State*, from *Love*. This represents amazing potential and helps explain, from the personality's perspective, the purpose for getting *Enlightened*. *Enlightenment* is the beginning.

# The Purpose of Enlightenment

The highest purpose of *Enlightenment* is for the spirit to return to *The Source*, it is the drop of water returning to the metaphoric ocean.　　But what ever happens above has a vibrational consequence below and so there exist reasons for *Enlightenment* on all levels.　　From the soul's perspective *Enlightenment* and liberation of the spirit raises the soul's vibration out of the karmic wheel of birth and death, raising it from the $6^{th}$ to the $7^{th}$ Dimension.

But what of the personality, comprising the mind, emotions, body and all the subtle vehicles within the lower manifest dimensions, those bodies which were present before the journey was even began? There are several ways that you can interact with, and benefit from the state of *Enlightenment*.　These also apply to some extent to the potential you have after first initiation and also second initiation, both of which are vast in comparison to the lower vehicles.

# Enlightenment Provides Ultimate Perspective

One of the ways you can really benefit from having completed your spiritual journey, and even from the moment you are first initiated, is by gaining a deeper perspective on what your spiritual nature is and thus what life is.

Before initiation a person who either practices meditation or is born particularly sensitive can be aware within the subtle planes of awareness right up to but not beyond their crown chakra. Some of these vibrational planes are vast and amazing, like the higher mental or the intuitive, also known as the Buddhic plane. However these vast planes are tiny in comparison to the higher spiritual dimensions revealed upon first initiation. Life experience and awareness before initiation is primarily centred around mind and emotions, both of which are anchored to the physical body.

Upon accessing spiritual dimensions well beyond the realm of feelings and thoughts you can explore a state of being which has nothing to do with your mind, body, emotions, and personality. This spiritual you cannot suffer or be killed and is free of fear. You just experience *Love* and peace on a level your mind and emotions can never fathom. The lower self is always contained and supported by these greater states and upon *Enlightenment* your spirit is beyond time, beyond a beginning or an end. You are life. You are *Love*. You are divine. Once you know your true nature it really provides a lot of perspective on "normal" life down in the lower dimensions of manifest creation. Nothing is taken away or diminished, you will still have a mind, emotions, and body, but what you now know yourself to truly be is so much more. The lower self is supported by your true nature which is divine.

There is only one state of *Enlightenment* so when two different people have realised *Enlightenment* then it is the same state. The experience and realisations of this state will be filtered down through your spiritual vehicles and into your lower vehicles, which do differ from someone else's and so the way *Enlightenment* benefits you may be different from someone else. Since *Enlightenment* is *Love* and everything that comes from it is *Love* in the form of spiritual energy, then the effect is always to provide the potential to raise your vibration. Some people will lose their fear of death or see through the illusion of the universe and have a sense of levity and joy, understanding creation to be a place supported by and created by *Love*. It depends on your mind and emotions but irrespective you will have the potential to live a life of true *Love*.

Whatever you realise about the greater states will provide more perspective on life within your lower vehicles and has the potential to remove fear and negativity in life. You can be in the world but less touched by it and that is the vibration of freedom within duality.

Perspective is the result of the contrast between the illusion of your manifest world and the great spiritual states culminating in *Enlightenment*. Without contrast there can be no realisations and it is having the vehicles on spiritual dimensions which are given during spiritual initiations, which allow you to explore the spiritual realms. The contrast of these realms provide the realisations that allow you to understand the true nature of your spiritual self and these different dimensions.

# Seeking Truth Through Exploring and Realisations

Contrast leads to realisations. Imagine that there is constant sound, never any silence. How would you know silence? Now imagine the sound suddenly stops, you would become aware of silence because of the absence of sound. Silence is the opposite of sound and it is their contrast that creates realisations about both sound and silence.

In the same way if everything was light then you would not notice light. But if there is darkness first and then light arrives, you would notice the light because of its contrast to darkness, its opposite.

It is only through contrast which exists because of duality that you can become aware of the nature of something. You can not learn about stillness without movement, nor darkness without light, or heat without cold. The manifest creation is total contrast allowing for your soul to learn.

The 8th Dimension down to our manifest dimensions of lower

vehicles are within duality. Only the 9$^{th}$ Dimension is *Unity*, being pure *Love*. On every level within this duality there exists the opportunity for realisations, the faster the vibration of the dimension then the closer the realisations are towards the nature of *Love*.

Initiation provides you the opportunity to be aware in these spiritual dimensions from the 4$^{th}$ Dimension to the 8$^{th}$ Dimension. As you notice the contrast within a dimension, then the vibration of the resulting realisation flows down until it crystallises in your mind which interprets and communicates the understanding to your lower vehicles and personality. Your mind is not at the same vibrational level as the actual realisation and did not make the realisation, however it allows understanding to "come down" to you from the higher vibrations.

Spiritual energy flows from the fastest vibration in the 8$^{th}$ Dimension to the slowest vibration in the 1$^{st}$ Dimension, which is why the realisations on the highest dimensions are able to flow down to the mind on a lower dimension. The physical world manifestation of the flow of energy is seen when heat moves from something hot to something cold, or when light pervades darkness.

Initiations gives you access to the higher dimensions and regular meditation builds your ease and ability to be present within these dimensions. Everyone is different and you may quickly progress through the different stages becoming *Enlightened* in days, months, or years. It depends on the individual. It is sometimes seen as a miracle and a positive thing if a person gets to *Enlightenment* quickly. In such a case the person has presented minimal resistance to the *Light Wave* and *Master Principal* so their spirit has been taken back to *The Source* quickly. This happens when the person is at ease in letting go of their attachment to their lower vehicles and is aligned with *Love*, with an open heart. The task now for a person who makes the realisations quickly is to practice letting go back into the different levels so that they can bring down more realisations about the nature of each of the dimensions. If they do not then they will still be *Enlightened* but there will be little in the way of realisations for their personality and mind to recognise and express this amazing state with.

The meditations during which you receive first initiation, second initiation, or *Enlightenment* are very special and are often referred to as "going through state changes". During these mediations the *Master Principle* guides your awareness through the different levels of the spiritual realms you now have access to, revealing the highest vibration available. For example on first initiation the *Master Principal* guides your awareness beyond your crown chakra and into the $4^{th}$, $5^{th}$, and $6^{th}$ Dimensions. How much you notice during this process really depends on your ability to let go of your attachment to your lower vehicles and to be present. Even a person who notices very little has still been given the ability to be present on these higher dimensions. After receiving each initiation meditation becomes about learning how to let go of attachment and to explore the higher dimensions revealed. Practicing letting go makes it easier because the more time you spend within each dimension the more you strengthen your presence on each dimension. Some people refer to this as "growing into your state", so that even years after an initiation you may still be having realisations from the higher dimensions.

Remember the spiritual dimensions are immensely more vast than the lower dimensions and there is not enough time in your life to experience every single aspect of these dimensions. A spiritual journey is about transcending all the dimensions until the spirit is free of duality. From your personality's perspective it is important to find the balance between attaining *Enlightenment* and building a strong presence and connection to every dimension. The more you have grown into your state and strengthened your connection to your state, the more able you are to integrate your different states of consciousness into your life.

## How do you Progress on a Spiritual Journey?

After you have received first or second initiation you must, within your meditation, be aware of and notice the spiritual *Light and Sound Energy* as this is the emanation from the *Master Principal* taking your awareness higher. The initiation provides the ability to be present within the higher dimensions but these dimensions are so vast that guidance is needed. The *Light and Sound Energy* is your guidance, helping you to grow into the higher dimensions revealed on initiation. The *Light and Sound Energy* works to constantly direct your attention towards the highest vibration and eventually to pure *Love, Enlightenment.*

## Stop Your Ego Getting in the Way of Meditation

There is a saying which is that "you don't meditate on the *Light and Sound*, it meditates on you". This is an attempt to explain that it is not by "trying", "demanding", "striving", "pushing", or "expecting" that you let go into meditation and progress.

To "try" is to put effort in where none is needed.

To "demand" is to suggest you are special.

To "strive" is to suggest you know where you are going.

To "push" is to attempt to force your limits into that which is limitless.

To "expect" means you think you know what is waiting for you.

These are all facets of the ego. It is by diminishing the ego and offering minimal resistance that you can progress more easily.

- Instead of "trying to meditate" you "surrender to your meditation".

- Instead of "demanding to progress" you become "grateful for the chance to progress".

- Instead of "striving to notice things" you "yield to what is before you".

- Instead of "pushing into stillness" you allow yourself to be "pulled back into stillness".

- Instead of "expecting things to be a certain way" you allow yourself to "accept what already is".

But how do you diminish your ego? The ego is a part of you, and it is the natural consequence of your personality. To hate it, attack it or criticise it is to hate, attack, or criticise yourself. Although it

**116**

can get in the way of meditation and channelling, it is still a part of you. Living a life of *Love* means loving unconditionally, and thus accepting everything without judgement. This includes accepting your ego. So be gentle and loving towards yourself. Imagine bringing your ego into the light. Every time you notice you are acting from your ego simply stop, forgive yourself, become a little stiller, reconnect with *Love* and then come from the stillness. The more you practice coming from a stiller place, the more you are practicing coming from *Love,* and the less you are practicing coming from ego. Eventually the habitual ego responses will diminish, because habits only survive when unchallenged.

## Spiritual Light and Sound Energy Guides Your Spirit

You may find that upon initiation you become more aware of your *Spirit Guide* which is a beautiful thing for both your *Spirit Guide* and you. Your spiritual journey may slow down though if you mistake communicating with your guide for meditating on the

*Light and Sound Energy.* Only the *Light and Sound Energy* which comes from the *Master Principle* can guide your spirit back to *The Source.* While it is fantastic to communicate with and channel your *Spirit Guide*, until you are *Enlightened* you must make your spiritual progress your priority. Your *Spirit Guide* is there to guide your soul along its life lessons. The *Light and Sound Energy* is there to guide your spirit along its spiritual journey back to *The Source.* Once *Enlightened* you will have complete freedom to explore every single level and to more easily communicate with *Spirit Guides* and beings.

Before *Enlightenment* it is down to each meditator to find the right balance between exploring and progressing. The more you trust the *Light and Sound Energy* then the more both exploring and progressing happen together.

Within *Light and Sound Energy* meditation you may find you perceive light more easily than sound, or the sound easier than light. However it is important that you perceive both as they have different qualities and roles. The sound vibration is what moves your awareness to higher dimensions, while the light communicates the nature of where you are. Your meditation teacher should be able to help you to meditate on both the light and the sound vibrations.

## *Meditation on Light*

There are different ways of "looking" on the inside and sometimes a person can hold themselves back by "trying to see". Explore what happens as you change from "looking for light", to simply "observing what is present on the inside". Not all light is visible, not all light is obvious, so do not go looking for what you experienced in the past or what you imagine you should see. Instead be open to noticing what is present in the moment. Often people fail to notice what is there because of their expectations of what should be there.

Whatever you give your attention to you get more of, so even the most subtle of light may lead to amazing realisations when you observe it without judgement. To observe without judgement is to accept and *Love* what is in front of you. The more you *Love* the light the easier you will find it, since *Love* removes the barriers to being present and aware. Enter meditation without expectation or desire and be present within the moment, loving what is in front of you.

When first learning remember it is the contrast which allows you to notice things so a good practice, when learning, is to notice the contrasts:

- Is it light or dark?

- Is it moving or still?

- Is there colour or no colour?

- Is it uniform or are there differences?

- Is it changing or staying the same?

- Is it all around you or just in one place?

- Is it three dimensional or flat?

- Is one place stiller than another?

- Are you separate from what you perceive or connected?

These questions can help you become more aware of your inner experience when learning to meditate. Ultimately though the questioning comes from the mind and you must leave the questions behind.

## *Meditation on Sound*

Like light, sound vibrations exist on every dimension within duality and so you may be aware of sound vibrations even before initiation. Once initiated you may notice new vibrations and also more kinaesthetic sensations associated with the sound. To explore how to meditate on the sound you can notice what happens as you tune in to different vibrations:

- Is there one sound or many?

- Where does the sound come from?

- How does the sound make you feel?

- What happens as you move your awareness into the

sound?

- Is there are relationship between the light and the sound?

If you are not hearing the sound then notice if you are feeling the sound vibrations. Just as "looking for light" gets in the way of seeing light then "listening for sound" can get in the way of being aware of the sound. Rather than trying hard to hear the sound, allow yourself to let go into the sound or the silence, as if you are lowering yourself leaning gently backwards into a comfortable bath, bathing yourself in the vibrations. It may help to bring your awareness gently into your brow chakra too.

When not meditating you may want to practice being aware of sound by listening to music. Choose a piece of music which you really enjoy, and that is positive in vibration, and then relax as if to meditate with your eyes closed. As you listen to the music allow yourself to really let go into the music, loosing yourself within the sounds, spaces and movement of the music. This is not meditation but it is good practice. By practicing letting go and loosing yourself in the music you are practicing loving. Since to give yourself completely to something is to love it. As with the light, practice the art of loving the sound vibration. Never judge it, even if you only hear a little you are hearing the flow of spiritual energy which comes from *The Source*, allow yourself to feel the joy of that understanding.

Although light and sound are being discussed as separate things here, you naturally may experience both the light and sound together. Discovering how they are related is one of the realisations you can enjoy within your spiritual journey.

## Become a Channel For Love and Light

Once you have finished your spiritual journey and realised *Enlightenment* then this is really where the magic begins. *Enlightenment* is the end of the spiritual journey but the start of living as a complete multidimensional spiritual being. You are now present on all dimensions, with your spirit returned to *The Source,* your soul free from the karmic cycle of life and death, and your lower vehicles and personality supported by the spiritual energy flowing down from *Love*. Imagine that *Enlightenment* is the reservoir of pure *Love*, the spiritual dimensions are the pipe connected to this reservoir and your personality is the tap. If you learn how to open the tap then *Love* as spiritual energy can flow down through all the levels and you can channel it into manifest creation.

Your spiritual journey was about raising your vibration to set your spirit free and reconnect with *God, Enlightenment, Love*. Channelling is using that connection to bring the highest vibrations down into the lower dimensions. Channelling can be the channelling of *Love*, light, healing, or information. For many people the term "channelling" refers to mediums who "channel" the soul of departed people. Channelling as described here is referring to much higher form. Spiritual dimensions which an initiate or *Enlightened* person have access to are in spiritual realms which include the soul realm but also go much higher. Since energy flows down from the fastest vibration to the slowest vibration creating the principle of "as above, so below" then the reason mediums are able to channel the departed is because it is the lower vibrational equivalent of an *Enlightened* person channeling light or *Love*. Everyone has a connection to their *Spirit Guide* and *Light Being* and once initiated it can become much easier to be aware of them.

## How Do You Channel?

For you to consciously channel something you require three things:

1. **Connection:** You must be connected to that which you wish to channel. The *Master* can channel the *Master Principle* because he is connected to the *Master Principle*. Someone who is *Enlightened* can channel the highest vibrations of *Spiritual Energy* because they are those vibrations.

2. **Intention:** You must have the intention to channel. Since intention is thought, which is faster than emotions, then

having the intention creates a similar emotional vibration, which in turn sets up the physical vibration. There is a saying "energy follows thought" so when you have the thought to channel then channeling starts. Intention is metaphorically "turning open the tap" to allow the faster vibrations you are connected to, to flow through you.

3.  **Vibration:** In order to be a powerful channel you need to have vibrational congruency with what you are channelling. This means that if you want to channel *Love,* then you must be in a loving vibration. The highest aspect is *Love* which is neutral since it accepts everything and is balanced. Since channelling is bringing faster vibrations down through the lower vehicles of the personality then the more neutral you are, the less resistance to the flow of these higher vibrations you present.

To consciously channel requires intention but once you are initiated and more so upon *Enlightenment* you may also be an unconscious channel since the crown chakra remains open provided you meditate or channel regularly. There are a number of people at this time who having attained *Enlightenment* are constant channels for *Love* or light. This is the role chosen for them by the *Ascended Masters*. They can of course act as conscious channellers too.

Your connection to spiritual energy is via your crown chakra, which is only opened when you receive initiation. When channelling spiritual energy it flows in through your crown and then flows through your meridian energy system without touching your lower chakra system. Meridian channels are the conduits for your energy but are also used for channelling higher vibrations.

## What are you Channelling?

You can channel *Love*, light, healing, and information. Each has a different vibration and yet all come from *Love*.

## Channelling Love

Absolute *Love* in its purest form is *Unity* and is the cause of everything and every vibration, so when you channel *Love* you bring the highest vibration possible within this dimension. *Love* reconciles opposites, it rebalances, it heals, it accepts, it forgives, it does not judge. It is the pure creative potential energy behind everything. When you channel *Love* it raises the vibration of the focus of your attention.

Because *Love* is everywhere and behind everything then anyone, whether initiated or not can channel *Love,* however you can only channel the vibration of *Love* up to the vibration you have access to. So someone who is initiated can channel *Love* at a faster, purer vibration than someone who is not. With each initiation the amount of *Love* you can channel increases too. The amount of Love you can channel is proportional to the size of your crown chakra.

## Channelling Light

It is important to understand that *Love* and light are two different things. *Love* is the source of light and light has a different vibration. In channelling light you are channelling the spiritual intention of spiritual intelligence. The goal is the same as *Love,* to raise the vibration of the focus of your attention. The subtle difference is that light has spiritual intelligence and so acts with intention, whereas *Love* is neutral and does not actively cause change but rather just accepts and provides neutral energy.

As with *Love* you can only channel the light from the dimensions to which you have access so if you aspire to be a light worker you must be initiated in order to channel spiritual light. The amount of light you can channel is proportional to the size of your crown chakra and upon *Enlightenment* you can channel the entire range of light from the highest aspect of light within the 8th Dimension. Unlike *Love* light is not found within *Unity* since it has a vibration and a form, and hence upon *Enlightenment* the amount of light you can channel is not increased compared to second initiation.

Because the energy you meditate on to receive the grace of *Enlightenment* is both light and sound then you may naturally ask "can you channel sound?". Sound can only be channelled into yourself, and cannot be sent to others.

## Channelling Healing

Often people ask about sending healing. Healing works in the lower dimensions as that is where there is imbalance. There is no healing in spiritual dimensions because there is no imbalance. Healing vibrations originate within the *Spiritual Hierarchy* and *Spirit Guides* can work with you to facilitate and direct healing. Since healing exists in the lower dimensions then you can send healing, even before receiving initiation. Once initiated you will be able to send more powerful healing. Upon second initiation your potential to be a healer increases, and it increases again once *Enlightened,* once *Enlightened* it is more efficient to do remote healing than hands on healing.

Channelling healing is instinctive and comes from a desire to help others. It is an expression of *Love,* but before you begin to send someone healing you must check that it is appropriate to do so. Sometimes the problem a person needs healing is part of their life lesson or life plan. Sometimes it is because of karma. It may also be there to present them with a chance to learn how to heal themselves. Before giving someone healing it is best to ask your *Spirit Guide* if it is appropriate to do so. If you experience resistance when trying to send someone healing then it means you are not meant to do so.

Some forms of dis-ease are caused by negativity in a person. Negativity can manifest as physical, emotional, or psychological imbalances and problems. Examples would include someone who is suicidal or extremely depressed. Connecting to someone who is suffering from a negativity based problem can be damaging to your own balance. When you have the desire to heal you open your heart chakra which demonstrates the principle of *Love*. Negativity is the absence of *Love*.

In order to help someone who has a negativity based problem it is best if you channel light with the intention to help them become more positive. When channelling light avoid being judgmental or trying to impose your ideas on what they should do or how they should change. Aim to stay neutral and simply send light to help them become positive. The intelligence in the light will take care of directing the energy in the way that helps the recipient.

You are all powerful healers when you have an open heart and the intention to heal another person or even the entire planet.

## How do You Channel Love, Light, and Healing?

Remember that you need a connection, intention, and vibration. Sitting comfortably upright as if to meditate with your legs uncrossed and not touching.   Place your hands palms facing upwards with your hands open.  The hands should not be touching each other but they can rest on your legs.

Keeping your eyes closed allow yourself to become stiller and neutral, without judgement, expectation or bias.   If you feel it would be helpful then bring your attention to each chakra in turn starting at the base chakra and moving to the crown chakra.   At each chakra have the intention to be balanced and open.   Once you feel more open and balanced then, with humility, ask your *Spirit Guide* to help you and to check whether it is appropriate to proceed with the channelling.

If you feel a block or get a sense of "no" then you can choose a different target for your attention. For example if you wanted to heal a person but you got the feedback it was not meant to be done, then send your healing to someone else or even to the planet as a whole. The target of your channelling can be any individual, thing, situation, animal, plant, location, or even your lower self. Equally it could be a collective like all whales, or all animals, the planet, the universe, all of humanity.

Bring your attention to your crown chakra and if you are initiated then you may notice light and sound. Allow the energy to be present. If you do not notice light and sound then that is perfectly fine too. You can then imagine the energy, whether it is *Love*, light, or healing to emanate from your palms and towards the focus of your attention. With practice you may feel the energy without imagination.

Do not mix what you are channelling, if you intend to channel light then just channel light. If you want to do more than one thing then do one at a time. When you first start you may not notice or be aware of anything and that is perfectly normal. When you are humble and coming from the heart then you will have trust that things are channelling even if you are not aware of it. This is because energy follows thought and if you have a strong intention then things will happen. With practice you may become more aware.

Remember it is important to be vibrationally congruent. If you attempt to channel for your own gain or agenda then you will not be congruent with *Love* and so you will get in the way of the channelling. There is no place for the ego in the act of channelling. Be positive in your choice of intention, instead of trying to block, limit, prevent, or attack the focus of your attention, be neutral and demonstrate unconditional *Love*. Do not try and use channelling to change someone or something, instead have the intention to help them to heal, rebalance, and realign with *Love*. Every soul matters and everyone is on the spiral. Always demonstrate unconditional *Love*, humility, gratitude and respect for *The Source* of energy and *Love*.

## Channelling Energy in a Group Versus Alone

When one *Enlightened* meditator sits for 10 minutes and channels energy in the form of light or *Love* then they channel a certain amount, which metaphorically you could say is 1kg of energy. If 20 *Enlightened* meditators sit at different times and channel the same energy for 10 minutes then they each also channel 1kg of energy metaphorically, and so there would have been 20kg of energy in total. If those 20 meditators now sit together and channel for 10 minutes at the same time working as a group then they would channel 20kg of energy. Meditating together does not result in more energy being channelled.

When channelling at the same time as a group either physically together or spread out around the planet the potential amount of energy channelled is the same as if each person had channelled independently. What does makes a difference when working as a group is human nature, because by channelling as a group you may feel more supported and motivated, helping you to maintain your focus and neutrality resulting in you channelling more energy than if you had been on your own. It is also a powerful statement of intent because when people cooperate together to channel energy it makes an inspiring symbolic representation of the principle of *Love*.

Another advantage to group channelling, especially if you are physically at the same location is that if there are people at different stages of their spiritual journey, say some at first and some *Enlightened*, then when they work together the *Enlightened* meditator's aura will support the less experienced meditators auras making it easier for them to stay focused and open up to their full potential. This is also true of group meditations in general where someone who is first or second may experience being "supported" by the energy of an *Enlightened* meditator.

It is important to understand that you are just as empowered when you meditate and channel energy on your own as you are when doing it in a group. What is most important is that you channel *Love* or light into the world regularly. Ideally to help heal the planet and reduce the negativity in the world at this time you would channel energy for at least ten minutes every day, but if you can do more then that would help more. If 10 minutes is too much then even 1 minute will make a difference. If channelling or meditating in a group with others helps you to maintain focus then it is worth doing. Socially it can be very supportive too and help people stay motivated. But you are under no pressure to channel or meditate with others. Perhaps your life schedule doesn't allow it or you don't know other channellers to work with. All that matters is that you do channel. When you channel energy not only does the focus of your attention benefit but you also benefit as you are practicing opening up your awareness to *Love*.

When channelling healing energy which is a different vibration from light and *Love,* working in a group can be more powerful than working individually. This is because most healing involves using energy to overcoming energy blocks or imbalances and by working together there is a higher amount of healing energy arriving at the same time than if it is spread out over time.

## *Channelling Information*

In everyday life, you get information in many different ways: what you see, what you hear, what you feel, and even what you taste and smell. The lower dimensions express the principles of the higher dimensions and so you can also get information in many ways on higher dimensions. When channelling information you are not bringing energy down and then transmitting it out to another person or thing, as you may do with healing, light, or *Love*, instead you are bringing information down into your lower vehicles so you mind can understand the information. Of course once you have it in mind you can then share it with others.

It is important to understand that you are channelling information from intelligence on higher dimensions, in other words you are communicating with part of the *Spiritual Hierarchy*. When channelling information it is good to start with the intention to channel from a specific source, for example your *Spirit Guide*, who is constantly there waiting for you to channel them so they can guide you. You can ask your *Spirit Guide* to help you.

Channelling brings information down to the mind plane which is also the same vibration as imagination. The challenge when you channel is to remain connected and neutral throughout. You may start a channelling session fully connected, however your ego and imagination can easily come to dominate your attention. This is simply the nature of the mind, but with practice and humility you can learn to more easily maintain the connection. It is also vital that when channelling you let go of any preconceived ideas, emotional attachments, or desires about the outcome. Desire, attachment and expectation are aspects of the lower self, the ego, and they will block the flow of information.

Because channelling requires neutrality to let go of desire, ego, and imagination then it is best done in a similar approach to meditation, although you may have your eyes open, especially if dowsing.

## Dowsing

Dowsing is a very good way to learn to channel information as there is a tangible interaction in the form of a pendulum. Typically dowsing is carried out using a free swinging pendulum suspended by one hand.  Some people place the other hand palm facing upwards just below the pendulum so it swings above their palm.  There is an energy centre in the middle of the palm and you may sense the pendulum as it swings over your upturned palm.  But whether you hold the pendulum over your palm or not is a personal choice as it does not affect the ability of the pendulum.

Start by calibrating the pendulum to swing one way for "yes" and to change motion for a "no".  For example it may swing in an anti-clockwise circle for "yes" and then change to a straight line for "no".  Whatever you want is fine so long as it is easy to differentiate the two.  You do not need to try and change the swing of the pendulum, simply hold it so the pendulum is free to swing and have the intention for your *Spirit Guide* to work through the pendulum. If the pendulum is not swinging much then ask your *Spirit Guide* to make the message stronger.

As you focus on the pendulum and maintain the most neutral, humble, and open state possible you can ask questions and notice how the pendulum changes. You can ask the question out loud or in your mind. Make sure the questions would have a simple yes or no answer. If you are not sure of the answer coming back then refine the question to make it simpler. You can also ask your *Spirit Guide* to make the movement of the pendulum more clear and if needed. Ask the question several times.

As you practice with the pendulum you will be strengthening your ability to channel and also your relationship with your *Spirit Guide*. Always remain humble and respectful as these are the qualities that keep the ego out of the way. What you may begin to notice is that as you are asking a question you will not only get the "yes" or "no" answer from the pendulum but you may also get additional information directly. It is not uncommon for an experienced dowser to say that their *Spirit Guide* is telling them which questions to ask in order to guide them towards the information that will help them.  This is the person becoming clairaudient, as they are hearing their *Spirit Guide*.

The more you use the pendulum the more you may sense the "yes" or "no" response in some way before you actually get a change in the pendulum.  This is you becoming more clairsentient as you feel the information.

## Clairaudience
The experience of hearing your *Spirit Guide* or any other spiritual being is known as clairaudience.  Since it is communication based on hearing then in order to develop clairaudience ability you can practice "listening" to your *Spirit Guide* and also communicate with them by "asking" questions with your inner voice thus having a conversation with them.  Sit in meditation but don't go too deep as you want to be able to ask questions with your mind. As with dowsing become neutral and let go of expectation, desire, emotional attachment, and become as aligned with *Love* as possible.  With respect and humility ask to communicate with

your *Spirit Guide.* You may hear an answer or you may get a feeling (clairsentience) or see something (clairvoyance) so be open to any form of communication.

Often when you first start channelling in this way you may naturally struggle to trust whether it is genuine channelling or simply your imagination. To help you can also use dowsing to verify the information. Some people will sense *Love* or joy when receiving channelling in this way since they are becoming connected with beings on higher levels which are beings of *Love.*

## Clairvoyance

Clairvoyance is seeing information and how you experience this will depend on which vibrational vehicle you are coming from. The lower form of clairvoyance is to see the information from the vibration of your mind. Although you are channelling beings from faster vibrations you only notice the information when the message has slowed down to a vibration which matches the vibration of your mind. The information would appear to you as images or even like a short film, in which you see a scenario. It may be exact like a premonition or it could be more symbolic, leading you towards understanding.

The higher forms of clairvoyance are when you get information directly on the higher spiritual dimensions. In order for this to happen you need to be sitting within your faster vibrational bodies. This is more likely in deep meditation as the experience is from your spiritual body and not your mental body. During such a channelling experience you may see the actual being you are channelling or you may have revealed to you information in a way which has little to do with your mind.

## Clairsentience

Often as you connect with your *Spirit Guide* you may have physical sensations, typically around the head and crown chakra. But you may also notice sensations around or within your body. This is normal and is your *Spirit Guide* interacting with you. They may be giving you healing for example to balance a chakra. Experienced channellers describe that they notice how different *Spirit Guides* trigger different sensations allowing them to tell which *Spirit Guide* they are connecting with. Clairsentience is often experienced along with clairvoyance and clairaudience. You may experience it at any time too as it may be your *Spirit Guide* trying to establish communication.

## Direct Information

Before any communication triggers a thought which is based on language, or a picture which is based on geometry, colour and memory there is just the pure intention of the communication. This pure intention is the vibration of the information, prior to it being projected into the limits which the mind understands. This pure information is on a faster vibration than the mind. When you tune into the pure information rather than the projected version then you are channelling direct information. The mind is vital to bring information down into manifest creation so that it can be communicated with others. Without a mind to interpret the communication then there is nothing to witness the information.

However as you practice channelling you may experience "direct information" which does not need to be slowed down and understood by the mind. This is much more of an intuitive assimilation of the information. As you become aware of the direct information the higher vibrational bodies of your awareness resonate with the vibration of the information. You are then getting the information in a much purer form than waiting for it to crystallise into structures which your mind can process.

Of course once you have received this higher vibration information, which means you are using a higher vibrational vehicle than your mind, you can still allow it to slow down and be processed by the mind.

## How to Communicate with your Spirit Guide

Some simple guidelines and advice to help with channelling and communicating with your spirit guide.

1. There are three main factors which determine how easy you find the process of channelling information: A) How open your crown chakra is; B) how integrated you are with your spiritual states of consciousness; C) how much you can get your ego out of

the way.

A) Your potential to channel is proportional to the size of your crown chakra. As you expand with each initiation it becomes potentially easier to channel. It is also affected by your lower vehicles and your ability to be neutral and aligned with *Love*. Once you are *Enlightened* then you can strengthen your ability by channelling light or *Love* regularly as this improves your ability to remain neutral and connected on all dimensions, allowing information to flow down through all the spiritual vibrations and into the lower vibrations of your mind.

B) How integrated you are with your state relates to how much you have sat in meditation and let go into your states. The more you explore your states of awareness by meditating then the more ease you have in allowing information to be passed down through the different spiritual dimensions.

C) Getting your ego out of the way simply means being present, being humble and being aligned with *Love*. The more neutral you are the less you block the flow of information. The more neutral you are, which is to say the more coming from *Love* then the less your mind distorts or misunderstands the information. If you are not neutral for example if you have expectations about what the answer should be, or you are emotionally resistant to the information, then there is more chance that your mind/ego will manipulate the information you receive. When ego is present then you may choose to ignore information you don't like, or allow your imagination to take a small piece of information and expand it in the direction you imagined it should be, which may not be in the direction of truth.

2. If you are unsure whether the information is genuine or comes from your imagination then, if you know someone else who you trust and who is also able to channel, ask them to check the information. You would give them the same question and see if they get back the same information. You can also check yourself by having a break and channelling the same information at another time. Remembering to be as neutral as possible.

3. Because it helps to be neutral and aligned with love then it is often best to do channelling after meditation, since the act of meditation naturally leaves you more balanced, neutral, and aligned with *Love*.

4. The first initiation opens your crown chakra, which is further widened on second initiation and even more upon Enlightenment. At any point in your journey if you do not meditate regularly then your crown chakra will start to close. When you meditate on *Light and Sound Energy* your awareness moves up and out through the crown chakra, guided by the *Master Principle* which helps keep the chakra open. When you channel *Love*, light, or information you bring energy down through the crown chakra which helps to keep the crown chakra open. If you do neither then your crown chakra will start to close. First and second initiates must meditate regularly, and once *Enlightened* you must meditate and/or channel in order to keep the crown chakra fully open.

If your crown chakra does shrink then it is possible for you to expand it again.   You will need to meditate more often and importantly re-align with living a life of *Love*.   There is no punishment and the closing of the crown chakra is simply a consequence of not using it.   Remember the *Spiritual Hierarchy* who opened your crown chakra want you to rediscover you true nature and are always supporting you.   The *Spiritual Hierarchy* never turn their back on you, even if you turn your back on them. There is no judgement, only forgiveness within *Love*.

5. When channelling there are two approaches you can explore: A) having a question or B) being open to whatever comes.   Both can be practiced and often the former leads to the latter.

A) Having a question in mind when you are channelling is a great way to bring down information.   You must be willing to receive any answer and not just the one you expect or want, which is why it is so important to sit in unconditional *Love* and to let go of expectations.   Have your question and then let go of it and make yourself available to receiving the information.

B) You can approach channelling with the attitude of "being open to receiving any information which your Spirit Guide thinks would help you". This approach as before really requires a lot of neutrality and being in a state of acceptance. At the start of your channelling session, just have the intention to be open to the communication and be totally present as how you receive the information could be in any of the ways described above, such as clairvoyantly, clairsentiently, clairaudiently, directly or a combination of them.

6. It is important to be as specific and detailed as possible when channelling. Especially when dowsing or asking for information. Sometimes two people may appear to get conflicting information, or you may find what you channel contradicts at different times. For example: "Is it possible for someone to come back and incarnate after attaining *Enlightenment*?" - the answer is "yes". But if you ask more specifically "will most people come back after attaining Enlightenment?" the answer is "no". These two answers seem to be in disagreement but further questions and

channelling reveal that in order to return and incarnate after *Enlightenment* the soul must have become an *Ascended Master*. So both answers were correct but it is only with more specific questioning that the apparent contradiction is resolved.

When channelling you do so from behind the veil of mind and emotions where there is little clarity. The beings on spiritual dimensions sending the information do not have a mind and emotions and so have access to information with clarity. These beings will answer your questions with neutrality, so you must strive for clarity by asking more questions and being specific.

At any one time half your planet is in daytime and half is in nighttime. If you ask "is it nighttime?" the answer is "yes" because somewhere it is nighttime. If you ask "is it daytime?", the answer is still "yes" as somewhere it is daytime. You need to be more specific, for example "is it daytime in this particular location?" in order to avoid seemingly contradictory information.

If contradictions do arise they are just indicating that either more questions need to be asked or that the channelled information was not received as best it could have been. This is why it is very helpful when channelling to work with others and to all have the humility and neutrality to not be attached to the information you channel.

7. Be kind to yourself and do not judge yourself negatively if you struggle. When you channel you are learning to be neutral and align with *Love* in order to channel higher dimensional information. Because you are channelling that information through your lower vehicles which are slower and more limited, then there may be challenges. It takes practice to become neutral and the *Spiritual Hierarchy* want you to practice channelling. Humility is one of the keys. If you struggle then that is part of the learning experience. Remember that unconditional *Love* also applies to self so be kind to yourself.

8. Remember that any information that can be understood by the mind is limited compared to the reality the information describes. Channelling information about spiritual reality is not the same

thing as becoming aware of that spiritual reality. *Enlightenment* which is beyond limits could never be described perfectly and cannot be channelled. It is something you have to "be" rather than "understand". Until you are *Enlightened* you must make *Enlightenment* your primary goal. The mind will enjoy the act of channelling but channelling will not reveal your true nature. Only spiritual expansion by meditation on *Light and Sound Energy* can reveal your true nature.

9. Understand that the spiritual beings you are communicating with are all part of the *Spiritual Hierarchy*. They are all aligned with *Love* and because they have no mind, emotions, or ego then they are all in vibrational alignment. "They are one" and they all serve *Love*. Therefore there is no information from one part of the *Spiritual Hierarchy* which would disagree with information from another part of the *Spiritual Hierarchy*.

The source of channelled information is the *Spiritual Hierarchy* and the reason they channel information down is to help humanity benefit from the information by guiding people towards living a life more aligned with *Love*. Information can help set you free and your loyalty should be to truth as truth comes from *Love*.

10. Channelling is about being open to receiving information from spiritual beings. With practice it can be like having a conversation where you ask a question and get information back as an answer. It is the forming of a relationship between your mind and personality and your *Spirit Guide* on a much higher vibration. This is why humility is so important. Being humble helps you to sit in the neutral space where there is less ego. The ego aspect of you strives to make you special. It is your ego that thinks "because I am channelling I am special". This is why being humble is so important because humility diminishes ego. In contrast when you are humble you may think "I am grateful that I am channelling" and so you are more open, receptive, and present within the channelling experience. Ego can lead to complacency. Even when you are *Enlightened* demonstrate respect for the *Spiritual Hierarchy* because they were the ones that set you free, and you did not earn *Enlightenment*, it came

from ultimate compassion and kindness.

11. Channelling is establishing communication with spiritual beings on higher dimensions, which requires you to be an open, humble, neutral and non-judgemental recipient. These qualities are the qualities of *Love* which reduce the resistance caused by the ego and lower personality. Having a clear intention to embody these qualities is very powerful as energy follows thought. One way to set your intention to be such a channel is to pray to your *Spirit Guide*. Prayer in this way is not the repetition of words written by another person and this is not prayer as some people are taught in religion. Prayer is a genuine appeal from the heart to your *Spirit Guide* and has nothing to do with religious beliefs. When learning to connect to your *Spirit Guide* a prayer reinforces your intention, helping you to start the process of communication.

A genuine prayer allows you to enter into a more humble vibration and demonstrate that you respect the process and will respect the information which comes from *Love*. Being spiritually awake and channelling is not religion and the action of prayer came well before any religion existed. Whether you are religious or not does not matter as a spiritual journey goes beyond belief to reveal truth. Prayer comes naturally and it is the beautifully honest act of appealing to your *Spirit Guide* for guidance and assistance. Prayer helps establish the connection when you speak from your heart by shifting your vibration into humility, gratitude, respect and unconditional *Love*.

12. You must have respect for the information you are given. Not all information you channel is necessarily meant to be shared with others. It is worth checking with your *Spirit Guide* before you share information as sometimes what comes is only intended for you. Not everyone is at the same vibration and some people may not be ready for it. You may be given information which will help you or prepare you for a change or event which is coming, but is not necessarily meant for others. Respect the sacredness of the bond you have between you and your *Spirit Guide*. Channelling is not entertainment, it is your *Spirit Guide* helping

you to raise your vibration. This is also why over time what you channel may be expanded on in the future. Your *Spirit Guide* is giving you what you are ready for at this time, there may be more to come when you are ready.

If in doubt ask your *Spirit Guide,* and respect their guidance because they have a much bigger picture than you, even if you are *Enlightened*, as the part of you that does the channelling is not that which is *Enlightened*.

# What Will You Do Next?

The ultimate goal of a spiritual journey is to reach *Enlightenment* setting your spirit free and empowering yourself. From the perspective of the soul and personality within the lower dimensions *Enlightenment* can be the beginning of a life more connected with *Love*, empowered and fulfilling. The personality exists within duality where there is free will and so there is absolute choice in what you choose to do once *Enlightened*.

With each initiation you receive there is a massive expansion of spiritual awareness and your lower vehicles act as witness to the realisations which come down from your spiritual bodies in the higher dimensions. Each expansion is an awareness and vibrational expansion, and upon Enlightenment all awareness and vibration is transcended. Your mind is not elevated with each expansion and so does not understand or comprehend the states. However by channelling and meditating you can integrate much more with your expanded states of awareness. This integration occurs by channelling information down and by expanding your awareness to grow up into your state. The more you practice the more you benefit. Having attained *Enlightenment* you can, if you choose, embrace a more empowered role and higher purpose as you are truly a spiritual being. You now have the potential to be a channel of *Love*, light and healing. Every person who is initiated is making the world a better place simply by being connected to the spiritual *Light and Sound Energy* which flows from *Love*. When you consciously channel Love, light, healing or information down into manifest creation then you help even more to raise the overall vibration of creation and humanity within it. You become a beacon of *Love* and light. The key to embracing this potential is to work with your personality to foster within your nature gratitude, respect, unconditional *Love*, non-judgementalism, and humility.

## Gratitude and Humility

The difference between receiving a "gift" and receiving a "reward" can be easily confused. A "reward" is usually something you get as payment for something you have done, whether it was work, action, self-development, or change, and the reward is therefore a consequence of something. For example it is natural to believe that spiritual progress is a reward for the time and effort put into meditation. It is easy to see how the meaning of "gift" and "reward" can get confused. The word gift, is often used where "reward" is meant.

To further blur the distinction, gifts are often given because it is expected of the giver, who may have an obligation. An example of this would be when, on your birthday, someone gives you a birthday gift. They may well have genuinely given the present from their heart, however the timing of their gift giving was in response to or acknowledgement of an event connected with you, in this case, your birthday.

Of course it is nice to give and it is nice to receive, there is nothing wrong in rewarding people, but in reality, and without judgement, it is very rare that you actually "give". Similarly it is also rare that you actually truly "receive" a gift.

The true meaning "giving", when you really give from your heart, is to give without needing anything back. When you truly give then you do not even need recognition. It is only truly giving when there is no personal agenda. The purest expression of giving is when you do so simply to help the person to whom you are giving.

Obviously what is given can vary, and giving an object of value or giving your valuable time are of similar value. The ultimate gift you could give someone else is your total attention. If you really give our attention to someone or something, then you are giving everything. You are giving your life in that moment. Because when you give your attention completely, you, as in your identity, ceases to exist in that moment.

When you step outside of your thoughts, outside of your feelings, outside of your awareness of ourself and give it to something else, then your ego and personality are no longer there, you are truly "selfless" in that moment.

But most of the time giving is partly a "selfish" action. You may give to feel good, or give to reward someone, or give to appease your guilt.

## The Role of Giving on a Spiritual Journey?

In meditation you can practice and experience selfless giving of your attention to your inner world, beyond your thoughts. Becoming aware of the space between and around each thought, transcending your emotions, letting go of your body. In doing so you get closer to *Love*, which really is selfless awareness. In a similar way once you have access to *Light and Sound Energy* then you can give it your attention in meditation too. But how much do you approach meditation with a purely giving attitude? If you are looking to get something from your meditation, if you have expectations, desires, or needs then are you really giving 100% of yourself?

And what of "receiving"? If someone else or something else is selflessly giving its attention to you, then you are receiving that attention. You can receive and yet not be aware, for example when you were a young baby you may have received support, kindness, and attention given by a parent. As a baby you were not consciously aware of receiving, you just did. It was not your fault you were unaware, and there is no criticism either. It was simply the nature of being a baby, to not be aware of what was being received. So being unaware means that the when you were a baby you could not show gratitude. But your parent continued to give out of Love.

# What is Gratitude?

To be "grateful" requires conscious awareness that a gift has been received. Gratitude means that you are a conscious receiver of a gift. As you learn to give your attention, for example in meditation, then it brings you closer to Love, closer to neutrality, and closer to acceptance. The highest level of giving is the revelation of *Love*, when you are given spiritual initiation. Initiation really is a true gift because you do not earn it and it is not a reward. Initiation is the *Spiritual Hierarchy* on higher dimensions giving you the opportunity to escape from your limited awareness of your lower vehicles. To escape into the spiritual dimensions, is the greatest gift because it is not just the gift of life, it is the gift beyond life. Lives come and lives go. Your soul returns to the soul essence and then incarnates again to have another life. Each life is but a breath of your soul coming in and letting go, being born and dying. Yet this gift of initiation gives you who, like every single other person, is not perfect, who is flawed, the opportunity to discover that you are more and to ultimately discover that you are *Love*, which is perfect, which is flawless.

So the greatest gift is the gift of initiation, because without it there is no start to your spiritual journey. The journey to discover that you are that which has never been born and can never die. To discover that you are the cause of everything, and are beyond all things. To discover that you are *Love*, and are beyond belief, beyond idea, beyond comparison. This is real.

The *Spiritual Hierarchy*, the *Lords of Light* working with the *Ascended Masters*, make it possible for you to receive the gift of initiation, connecting you to spiritual *Light and Sound Energy* which leads eventually to *Enlightenment*. You for your part must learn to give your attention back to the *Light and Sound Energy*. What you have received is *Grace*, because you did not earn it and yet it is the ultimate gift of *Love*, beyond life. When you are initiated you will have been conscious of the process, having consciously received the initiation, and within that awareness there is the opportunity for gratitude, for you to be grateful.

**165**

But like every single person who lives, you have an ego and the ego always wants to turn to look down, through the layers of your lower vehicles, through your mind, through your emotions and onto your body. Whatever is received by you, you ego will turn and try to direct its attention inwards. But rather than inwards towards an expansion, the ego turns its attention inwards into a contraction, focusing more into the limited lower vehicles. In doing so the ego seeks to adorn the small with the great. To take the vast spiritual states of awareness revealed on first initiation, second initiation, and *Enlightenment*, and to try and use them to decorate the personality. As if to say "this personality is great because it has access to these great states". That is what the ego does. It is its nature. Your ego keeps you small by turning your back on the truth. Instead of you being aware of the light that shines from absolute *Love*, your ego turns you around to notice the metaphoric shadow that you cast in this light. Because when you sit within ego you do not face towards the light, you only see the shadow of your ego. The edges of your shadow define you.

When you are grateful, full of gratitude, full of grace, it keeps your attention turned towards *Love*, the source of the light. Though your ego still casts a shadow, you are facing into the light and so you see less of your ego and more of your truth. Being grateful means that you do not take for granted what you have been given, but rather you remain in awe of the gift. Being grateful means that your heart stays open, because the ego is smaller.

Whatever you give your attention to, you get more of and you nurture. So if you look at the shadow that your ego casts then you get more darkness and you get harder edges, as you notice the contrast between the edge of your shadow and the light around it. But if you turn and face the light, if you use being grateful to remain full of grace then you get more *Love* and your heart opens even more. Gratitude, gratefulness, these are just words, but what these words describe are an orientation of intent to stay focused on *Love*.

When grateful you do not reject a gift you are given, instead you remain open to it. You cannot be initiated or *Enlightened* because you think you are ready or you think you are worthy. Spirituality is never earned, it remains always a gift. The *Spiritual Hierarchy* who give this gift, want you to receive it and for you to realise that you are *The Source*, that you are *Love*. When you are humble and grateful then you are most ready. Similarly your teacher who is going to initiate you will also want you to be initiated, and if they are waiting then they are waiting for a reason. Sometimes it is practical considerations, and sometimes they are just giving you time to soften, to let go of expectations, to become more humble.

If you demand initiation it demonstrates that you are not really tuned in to your own humility and it is your ego demanding and saying "I am special, therefore I am ready". You have yet to fully understand that spirituality is not a reward but a gift.

If you do not embrace the gift when offered saying "I am not ready" then you have also not understood that spirituality is a gift. To reject the opportunity is to turn away the gift. So if your teacher wants to initiate you then trust you are ready and be grateful when the opportunity arrises. If you feel you are waiting then trust that your teacher does want you to progress, and there is a reason you have to wait.

If you are not progressing then it is either that you are not practically ready in which case your teacher can give you advice and guidance towards getting you ready for initiation. Or it is because your teacher is waiting for you to be in the right place in terms of humility, kindness, gratitude, respect, unconditional love and non-judgementalism, those love-oriented qualities which are not found in the shadow that the ego casts.

Gratitude, Humility, kindness, and an open heart are are nurtured in you when you are aligned with light and *Love*. So try not to judge yourself, because to judge yourself is not demonstrating unconditional love. To say "I am not worthy" is to question the *Divine Intelligence,* so if you are going to or have already received initiation then it is because the person initiating you believed you were ready. Be grateful. If you have been *Enlightened* it is because you were given the opportunity and you

169

gave your attention. Be grateful. In being grateful and showing gratitude you keep yourself aligned with *Love*. The "yourself" which is aligned is not that which is *Enlightened*, and it is not that which recognises itself in the stillness. It is your personality, those lower vehicles that were there before you took the first steps on your spiritual journey towards *Enlightenment*. The part that shows gratitude is that part of you which is host to your ego, which is not *Enlightened*, that is able to remain in duality. Gratitude is what orientates your lower self towards *Love*, towards *Unity*. Gratitude is a way of being, it is a choice, and it keeps your heart open, it keeps you present, helping you stay out of your ego by remembering that you were given a gift, that you were never ready for, but it was given anyway.

Everyone that walks this planet has a personality and an ego. The ego is not an evil thing, there to be punished or to be ashamed of. It is just the shadow that is cast when you look through your lower vehicles and identify with them. On a spiritual journey you are lucky since you have the opportunity to know that there is so much more, but the opportunity does not guarantee that you turn your attention towards *Love*, it just creates the potential.

To stay attuned with *Love*, practice being grateful towards the *Spiritual Hierarchy* who give this gift. Remember that even after *Enlightenment* it is *Divine Intelligence* which guides you. It is your Spirit Guide which continues to provide you with opportunities to continue your soul journey, to give that part of you that remains in duality, but on the higher spiritual dimensions the chance to evolve. Remember what you are, remember where you have come from, and remain grateful. Being grateful makes you both a channel for and a witness to *Love*. It makes you present in the moment and softens the ego.

It is ego which spoils the journey, which judges and has expectations, which demands and refuses. It is the ego which blinds you to the miracle that is in front of you. Gratitude is how you can free yourself from your ego.

Gratitude is a shift in orientation, a change in attitude which when

171

fostered will help you more reconnect with your heart and allow you to witness and channel *Love*.

You have a choice, you always have a choice, and when you are awake you can change.   You are love, you are loved, you can love.  Start with yourself and change the world.

The way back to the source truly exists and you may have the potential to attain *Enlightenment* at this time.

The question is "what will you do?"

**We are one**

# About the author

It is December 2016 and I am Mark Zaretti a meditation teacher based in the UK. My background is as a scientist studying Biology up to Masters Level. I work in IT during the day and I teach and support meditators during my spare time. I do

not charge for my teaching or guidance. The greatest pleasure is helping others on their spiritual journey, especially as I understand that we truly are all connected.

I have always questioned the world around me and wanted answers based on my own experience. I've always felt that there was something more to life. Perhaps you know what that is like? So I started meditating intuitively as a young child and by 1998 I was lucky enough to have been initiated into *Light and Sound Energy* meditation. I realised *Enlightenment* in 2009 after approximately 8000+ hours of meditation on *Light and Sound Energy*, but it wasn't until 2015 and several thousand more hours of meditation that I discovered that I could channel.

This coincided with the emergence of this *Light Wave* energy and the potential for myself and others around the planet to be able to pass the energy on and initiate people. This *Light Wave* is amazing and people just like you are now realising their state changes even quicker than before. What took me years is now taking people months, weeks or even days. It is a truly inspiring time to be on this planet.

The more I channelled then the more I started getting information which I realised could be helpful for people who are just starting out as well as those who have realised their *Enlightenment*. Much of the information I present here can help you to make sense of your journey and to understand better how to integrate with your spiritual nature as you progress. It doesn't matter if it all makes sense right now, or if some of it is challenging, I know because I've been there too! The more you explore your meditation the more you may understand and relate to the truth this information guides you to. Trust me your spiritual journey and finding out for yourself comes first. This book is like a map to help you figure out where you already are, and where you could go next.

So where did this information come from? What I share in this book is based on my direct experiences and realisations from over 34 years of meditation. I also draw on the experiences and understandings I've had from almost 20 years of teaching people. The majority of the book is channelled information, some directly by me and some shared with me by other *Enlightened* channellers. For the latter I would then verify all their information by directly channelling with my *Spirit Guide* and from higher beings within the *Spiritual Hierarchy*. Each bit of information would then lead me to channel even more to get the details.

There are many people to thank who have supported this work including those who have challenged me, motivating me to channel even more and to be even more specific. To all, you have my gratitude and thanks, as do my teachers from the past without whom I would not be in this position to help and serve others. I wish to thank the *Spiritual Hierarchy* too – thank you for your patience and guidance.

The challenge with this work is that it is never finished. Every channelled bit of information triggers even more questions and I want to make sure that it is captured as accurately as possible. If anything contradicts what you know from your own experience then it is a wonderful opportunity for you and I to ask more questions and to channel more information. Together we can make a more complete picture. For this reason I have labelled this "Edition 1". I know there is more information to come and there is also lots of information I've channelled which I cannot share at this time.

We are one, and together we are empowered. It is my sincerest hope that this book helps guide you and I encourage you to share it freely with others. I am not the source I am simply the messenger and if ever there was a need for humanity to rediscover its truly amazing nature then that time is now.

When you would like to know more or to find out how to start your journey meditating on spiritual *Light and Sound Energy* then please visit https://thewaybackmeditation.org and get in contact.


Wishing you peace, inner stillness, and a life of LOVE,

Mark x

# Postface

It is now November 2019 and the last couple of years since this book was first published on the 1st of January 2017 have been wonderfully transformative. Even while I was towards the end of writing the book above I was told by the Spiritual Hierarchy that I would be called upon to write a second book in the future.

Now the future is here and there are not one but three more books. Right now book two "The Way Back, The Six Virtues" is published and book three and four are written, but they will not be published for a few more years. "Why the delay?" Please be patient, and know that there are still events which need to unfold on the 3$^{rd}$ dimension and above before the information held within those two books can be known. There are many unseen things that must align but also humanity needs to spiritually evolve and mature and the good news is that in part this is down to you and you can make a difference. Whether you are initiated or just starting out, you are a vital part of this growth.

In the last few years I have retired from work in IT and dedicated my time to writing these next three books and teaching spirituality and meditation. To help facilitate this I have created a not-for-profit organisation to promote the teachings and insights gained from channelling and collectively this is known as "The Way Back Group".

To help reach as many people as possible I have produced over 60 guidance videos, channelled more articles and kept the website up-to-date with guidance and helpful advice, all of which is freely available. Importantly more people have been initiated and the light is spreading. This work continues and is supported by kind donations and the proceeds from the books. So thank you for your support, we are truly grateful.

The next books expand upon a lot of the information in the book above going into so much more detail with entire chapters dedicated to topics that only get a paragraph or a page above. In fact book three and four combined total over 390,000 words compared to the modest 30,000 in the book above.

Importantly those books explain how spirituality, your soul journey, life on Earth and indeed humanity fits into the much larger and quite honestly awe inspiring and humbling bigger picture. Very little of which has ever been known by humanity and certainly not by me until I embarked on this most recent step in the journey.

I would say that the book above covers about 5% of this bigger picture and I am truly humbled that the Spiritual Hierarchy entrusted me and a few others with the task of bringing this information to you, and also that you have been guided to this, the first book. I hope the next books also find their way to you when the time is right.

In the meantime I wish you peace, harmony and ultimately love, because in the end all there is is love.

Mark x

Printed in Poland
by Amazon Fulfillment
Poland Sp. z o.o., Wrocław